NEW ZEALAND IN A GLOBALISING WORLD

NEW ZEALAND IN A GLOBALISING WORLD

EDITED BY
RALPH PETTMAN

VICTORIA UNIVERSITY PRESS

VICTORIA UNIVERSITY PRESS
Victoria University of Wellington
PO Box 600, Wellington
www.vuw.ac.nz/vup

© Editor and contributors 2005

ISBN 0 86473 495 6

First published 2005

This book is copyright. Apart from any fair
dealing for the purpose of private study, research,
criticism or review, as permitted under the Copyright
Act, no part may be reproduced by any process
without the permission of the publishers

National Library of New Zealand Cataloguing-in-Publication Data
New Zealand in a globalising world / edited by Ralph Pettman.
Includes bibliographical references.
ISBN 0-86473-495-6
1. International economic relations. 2. New Zealand—Foreign
relations. 3. New Zealand—Defenses. I. Pettman, Ralph.
327.93—dc 22

Printed by Astra Print, Wellington

CONTENTS

	Preface *Ralph Pettman*	7
1	Analysts, Practitioners and Not Getting It Wrong: Some Implications for New Zealand's Foreign Relations *Roderic Alley*	9

New Zealand in a Globalising World

2	Deconstructing Globalisation *Alejandro Groppo*	29
3	The Marsden 'Globalisation and New Zealand' Project *Brian Easton*	37
4	Sovereignty, Globalisation and New Zealand Foreign Policy *Robert Patman*	44
5	Diplomatic 'Interests' *Malcolm McKinnon*	65

New Zealand's Role in the Pacific

6	Security in Oceania in the Post-9/11 and -Bali Era *John Henderson*	73
7	New Zealand's Role in the Pacific: The New Warfare State *Keith Suter*	83
8	The Concept of the 'Failed State': A Brobdingnagian View from Lilliput *Richard Herr*	99

9 Diplomacy, Politics and Nuclear Testing: 110
   New Zealand Confronts France 1995–96
   Stephen Hoadley

10 South-West Pacific: Arc of Instability or Matrix 119
   of Discontent?
   Jon Fraenkel

Trans-Tasman Relations

11 Looking Out from Down Under: Diverging World Views 141
   Terence O'Brien

12 Being on the Right Side of History 152
   Les Holborow

13 A Tale of Two Nation-States 156
   Damian Edwards

14 It's the Region, Stupid! 176
   Denis McLean

Contributors 184

PREFACE

On 5 December 2003, Victoria University hosted the Fourth Wellington Conference on World Affairs. This volume contains all but one of the papers from the conference.

The Wellington Conference on World Affairs is a biennial event. It is an academic conference that brings together scholars from around the country and from overseas to address a common theme in selected ways.

The theme for 2003 was 'New Zealand in World Affairs'. There were three panels, one on New Zealand in a Globalising World, one on New Zealand's Role in the Pacific, and one on Trans-Tasman Relations. This particular conference was special, however. It was held in honour of Dr Roderic Alley, who would retire early the following year. Dr Alley chose the conference title. He also gave the keynote speech, the text of which is printed here.

Dr Alley has had a long and distinguished career at Victoria University as a tertiary teacher and researcher. His address to the conference was entitled 'Analysts, Practitioners and Not Getting It Wrong: Some Implications for New Zealand's Foreign Relations' and is an outstanding example of the quality of his thought. It is the culmination of a lifetime's judicious reflection on the puzzles that global affairs present, and it will deservedly become a touchstone in New Zealand's attempts to make sense—academically, bureaucratically, and politically—of its place in world politics.

Dr Alley was introduced first by the vice chancellor, Professor Stuart McCutcheon, who on behalf of the university was pleased to thank Dr Alley for his exemplary service, and to testify to the extraordinary esteem in which his fellow scholars hold him. Dr Alley was introduced next by Sir Geoffrey Palmer, a one-time prime minister of New Zealand, who highlighted the lasting value of what Dr Alley has done for the community at large.

Most of the subsequent speakers prefaced their remarks with complimentary personal anecdotes, and vivid accounts of Dr Alley's contribution to the discipline and to their own careers. Taken together, these clearly document the breadth and depth of his intellectual influence, as well as the great regard in which he is held. These remarks are not reproduced here, but they were a notable feature of the proceedings of the conference itself.

The retirement of a scholar of Dr Alley's standing always evokes mixed emotions. On the one hand it is a pleasure to see such an exceptional co-worker being rewarded with the opportunity to move on to other things. On the other, there is the sadness of knowing that the next generation of students will not have the chance to benefit from his extensive experience and knowledge. There is also the sobering realisation that his wise counsel and willing hand will not be there to help the Political Science and International Relations Programme through the difficulties it must face in the years ahead.

Dr Alley leaves with the warmest wishes of the entire programme. It is hard to imagine a more able and esteemed colleague, or one who better exemplifies the best that his profession provides.

Ralph Pettman
Professor of International Relations
Conference Convenor

1

ANALYSTS, PRACTITIONERS AND NOT GETTING IT WRONG: SOME IMPLICATIONS FOR NEW ZEALAND'S FOREIGN RELATIONS

Roderic Alley

Introduction

This volume is about our capacity to make sense of a turbulent world, a challenge that for analysts and practitioners alike is immense, pressing and unavoidable. Analysts encounter an unresolved ambivalence about the capacity of International Relations as a discipline to fulfil this function, however, the subject continues to struggle, its head barely above parochial proclivities and seemingly sterile debates. Foundational approaches including liberalism inadequately explain situations of disadvantage, inequity and human suffering.[1] Practitioners by contrast, driven by timetables and resource constraints, concentrate on firefighting the tyranny of immediacy, the dry tinder of doubt, dissent and disapproval left unattended in the hope that it doesn't ignite.

For practitioners enhancing effective and timely judgement calls in a world of turbulence offers practical advantages. Vigilance, scepticism and consultation do reduce the error rate. This is no matter of micromanagement: small oversights, as any experienced bureaucrat might testify, can assume major consequences. The effective management and conduct of foreign relations is an unimpeachable objective, but I'm not sure if its prescription is the task of academics, any more than we might expect officials to visit us regularly, pencils at the ready, to grade the latest batch of student assignments.

A useful fusion of practice and discourse can occur through the critical interrogation of existing public tendencies, doctrines and beliefs. Should analysts quote to practitioners Robert Cox's widely cited dictum that theory 'is for someone and for some purpose', they may well agree. This is helped by inquiry about inquiry, and through a circumference that includes the companionship of history, an imagination born of empathy and, for public purposes, the avoidance of what David Hume once termed 'imprudent vehemence'.

Such interrogation confronts persisting public dilemmas about how to reconcile individual interest with collective good. Although nothing new for students of politics, the consequences of bungling that reconciliation are now fearful. Unequal power turns ugly when harnessed to some form of collective authority or linked to stable systems of interstate or intersocietal cooperation.[2]

Unaccountable and random violence has, in some instances, sacralised the fortress mentality of homeland security as the optimal public good, at least in the immediate term. Sovereignty's mental world has been reinforced, state borders being the ultimate arbiter of who is 'us' and who is 'them'; 'self' and 'other'; 'national' and 'alien'; 'believer' and 'infidel'. Such dualism can reinforce perceptual distortion, subvert political consensus, and impede the formation of independent rules needed to moderate interests by mediating them. Effective political judgement, I would submit, entails a close understanding of these dualisms and the languages that they employ. However, none of this is simple or straightforward: things go wrong for professors and practitioners alike once it's assumed that a short course version of these dilemmas will suffice.

Entry is possible, however, by considering three avenues of enquiry, all interrelating, and forming the basis for most of these remarks.

First, and for the purposes of order under equity and hopefully justice, why do norms, rules and standards-based conduct evolve to persist in some settings while in others the ultimate arbiter remains singular sovereign interest, backed if necessary by force—the world familiar to Thomas Hobbes? Are Caesar's divisions permanent, or can civilised rule make tame the interests of those keenest to exploit the risks of anarchy? Here we lack, but badly need, a plausible account about how to legitimise normative systems, including international law. I argue that ministering to the principles of reciprocity, deliberation and justification can facilitate that task.

A second focus looks to a major dilemma of our times: namely, whether a reconciliation of the sovereign interest and rule-governed international conduct is currently possible so long as that paragon of multilateralism after World War II, the United States (US), maintains a position where it risks becoming its pariah sixty years later? Is that tendency permanent, or can the United States resume the global citizen functions that marry its immense human capacity to international responsibility?

Third, how do we explain a world sorely in need of social order, but propagating practices that violate the principles of reciprocity, deliberation and justification needed to secure a durable order legitimised by a citizenship of sovereign consent? How much official discourse actively condoning such violation is tolerable? And where does this leave the global citizen aspirations of a small state such as New Zealand? These concerns are neither random nor nebulous.

Norms

To the first question, then, concerning the problematic development of norms and rule-guided conduct within the contemporary conduct of world affairs—norms we view as 'shared expectations about appropriate behaviour held by a community of actors'.[3] As they aid regulation so they help constitute state identities, New Zealand's standing abroad being defined by the seriousness with which it fulfils its normative obligations. Given their ubiquity, though, multiple norms may involve 'competing even contradictory prescriptions for behaviour and identity [making] it difficult to predict which norms will be most influential'.[4]

Pragmatists acknowledge that rules and norms shaping international political conduct are necessary, but bound by the contingencies of a sovereign state world. As the United Nations (UN) Charter legitimises collective action for enforcement purposes, so does it sanction actions claiming self-defence under Article 51. While the UN is an agent of intergovernmental activity in the service of states, it is also a framework for dealing with transnational problems and where common standards of humanity, not sovereign accommodation, constitute the overarching consideration.[5] There is evident tension here between rules offering general protection and sovereign interest, well highlighted for example in the 1996 Advisory Opinion of the International Court of Justice, a finding of immediate interest to New Zealand.

In its advisory opinion on the legality of the use or threat of use of nuclear weapons, the court found such use would generally be contrary to the rules of international law while failing to conclude that nuclear use would be unlawful in all circumstances—a recognition that, for the nuclear weapons states at least, a practice of nuclear deterrence exists and is adhered to regardless of humanitarian law clearly outlawing the deliberate targeting of civilians and preventing their unnecessary suffering. This was an instance, if you will, of the International Court ruling pragmatically.

Such a ruling indicated the limits of the capacity of the law to constrain demands driven by major political interests. But what else might constrain those interests? Realists offer scant comfort. They evince an ineluctable pessimism about reforming a state-based system, run according to the dictums of material self-interest and survival. Rather we must look to some bridging principles, the first of which is reciprocity.

Reciprocity
Reciprocity in international conduct entails indivisibility, general principles of conduct, and diffuse responsibilities. It lessens the costs of interdependence and may enhance its opportunities. Pervasive in premodern cultures, reciprocity binds relations between consenting states; unlike exchange or market relations, exit is not cost free so far as longer term advantages are concerned, a lesson that the United States is now learning over Iraq. Reciprocity enhances sovereign equality, smaller no less that stronger states being entitled to expectations of a faithful fulfilment of obligations by others. It offers insurance against the disposability of relationships on instrumental grounds by setting them within standards-based rules. This permits benchmarking, fresh agenda formation, and durable dispute settlement. In negotiating settings, reciprocity facilitates trade-offs, although that may not mean an equalisation of concessions. Kept in focus are principles of equivalence, fairness, contingency and responsiveness. Much of this sounds, and is, elementary. Apart from a minority of governments that are either non-functional or delusional, reciprocity in most fields is alive and well. Yet within significant areas of international security, potentially shaping the lives of billions of people, this is a principle that is in deep trouble.

In part, this is because reciprocity's national roots are not secure. Domestically, reciprocity is widely recognised as a core principle of democracy, through obligations that citizens owe one another via mutually binding laws and public policies that they collectively enact. Extraction without just redistribution has played out domestically through failures to institute graduated tax; reform property or land laws; or allocate values fairly under suffrage and representational systems. Deformed redistribution generates failed domestic conflict settlement—a multitude of local Versailles—and where reciprocating responsibilities and obligations have been neglected or distorted. That is magnified globally, when economic governance lacks the public consent required for its operational effectiveness.[6] The more that a body such as the International Monetary Fund, or for that matter the World Trade Organisation, intrudes into national affairs, the greater the requirement for the consent of, and accountability to, the citizens involved.[7] Evident conditions of violated reciprocity provide salutary reminders about the dangers of neglecting the long-standing concerns of politics—who does the suffering, and who the exploiting at another's expense.

Deliberation
A second function concerns deliberation. Deliberation to some purpose requires structures that are internationally legitimised and representative, and where conspicuous failure to accommodate deliberative activity incurs tangible costs to powerholders. Even if indirect, links to public governance functions whether by submissions to public officials, forms of petitioning, or the effective ventilation of grievance require durable and well-tended channels able to convey organised deliberation. External linkage permitting unhindered transnational deliberation is needed. Recorded deliberation constituting a public memory trail requires institutionalisation. This matters for the reconciliation of historical grievances. Effective deliberation can generate forms of knowledge creation independent of, but related to, the conduct of international relations. To function effectively, public deliberation requires news media systems that are not totally dominated by commercial return or conglomeration. Discounting the political dimensions of knowledge demeans its effectiveness as a tool of international collaboration.

However it is viewed against such criteria, the deliberative process is in difficulty. The growth of private authority systems, technical expertise, autonomous external bodies, and social movements have seen significant features of the democratic process undergo relative decline. This has eroded the significance of elections, the role of legislatures, and the functions of elected officials. In the United States the interests of campaign financing, public opinion polls, and television exposure browbeat the domestic political process.

Yet in a broader sense democracy is ever more important, whether through freedom's innate significance for human existence, or through its underrated deliberative and discursive practices uncovering knowledge employed for public purposes.

This can include the revisiting of foreign relations deliberation previously ignored or neglected. What is now termed the democratic deficit in foreign relations had important origins with the Union of Democratic Control formed in Britain at the height of World War I and that demanded stronger parliamentary functions in scrutinising the conduct of foreign relations. Those seeking the elimination of nuclear weapons look to the abolition of slavery for relevant deliberative knowledge. Some records of conference diplomacy involving non-governmental organisations determined to insert public deliberation into the conduct of foreign relations can convey a remarkable contemporaneity. In 1937, New Zealand's representatives participated in a Pan-Pacific Women's Association Conference in Vancouver. And what did they speak about?—the traffic in arms; population pressures; the traffic in women and children; labour standards; socialised health; and the development of educational programmes under rapidly changing economic and social conditions.[8]

Justification
A third dimension identified concerns justification. Governments, intergovernmental agencies, transnational corporates and non-governmental bodies avoiding international accountability find it harder to avoid statements of position. Enhanced means of electronic communication leave organisational representatives in no doubt that what they put on the public record matters. Statements of justification provide an identifiable location of responsibility that may in part counter secrecy and information massage. Even when rebutted, acts of justification assist future problem management. They put down markers providing comparison for subsequent actions.

Accountable justification helps disentangle propaganda from core objectives and assists towards better-grounded argument favouring particular courses of action. Even if offered on a 'take it or leave it' basis, mechanisms of justification utilised in the conduct of foreign relations can facilitate the necessary closer internal coordination. Consonance between policies followed, and plausible justification helps build external reputational influence, not least for small states. Once settled within international institutional routines, justification procedures can reduce the scope for strong states to step beyond them to exert bilateral pressure and threats against smaller powers.

Internally within the foreign policy process, an agency unprepared to have its position supporting or denying a particular course of action recorded should not be involved. Without due record of position, it is difficult to reconcile policy differences or authorise recommendations. We note the

United Kingdom Hutton inquiry in this regard.

Overall, acts of justification help people seek political agreement through principles that are defensible to others who share common aims of reaching agreement. This respects, not demeans, the capacity of individuals to reason self-consciously, self-reflectively and in ways that are self-determining.

Established modalities of public justification help to locate otherwise concealed sources of political influence. They can comprise private forms of authority generated by markets including major accounting services, as well as technical, supranational or citizen and popular forms of authority. A statement of justification by a government about what it's doing in foreign relations gives focus for dissent, and leaves publics clear about what they do not want. This applies to justifications supporting intervention—in whatever forms that may take.

Justification permits a plurality of options to gain audience, including the viability of alternative systems of governance. Opportunities emerge for mistrust to abate. Authority or standing to enter claims of justification legitimises autonomy. It involves the ability to deliberate, judge, choose, act and follow different courses of action in private as well as public life. This offers public exposure to any moral claim made in the conduct of foreign relations, whatever its nature or however disputed. Mutual justification requires reference to substantive values or what Rawls called fair terms of social cooperation. Whether as punishment or forgiveness, justification procedures are vital to post-conflict accommodation and reconciliation, their frustration or denial an invocation to future resort to force.

As an interim conclusion, then, I enter a claim that, for any government, attention to how these principles are operating either within the politics of other states, or in relations between them, helps reduce the risks of misjudging why mistakes are made.

The United States and multilateralism

The second major heading regards the indelible capacity of current United States foreign relations to complicate or confound principles of prudent judgement. A core puzzle is readily identifiable: of any nation, the United States currently has placed a massive investment in ensuring that others adhere to the obligations of international law and institutions. This American investment in workable international collaboration has been built up at considerable cost over several decades. It encompasses the interests of US companies, consumers, and combatants. Indeed any survey of United States interdependence reveals the extent to which the international community has moved down the often unspectacular but essential road of rule-based cooperation. Why, then, has an incautious unilateralism placed so much of this outlay in jeopardy?

For John Ruggie, multilateralism in its generic sense serves as a 'foundational architectural principle' from which American policy planners set out to reconstruct the postwar world.[9] This extends to the creation of organisations where the United States itself is not a major player. A condition of European receipt of Marshall Plan money, for example, was that the West Europeans create multilateral systems of cooperation among themselves, this leading to the formation of the European Payments Union. Significant as well was American support for the creation of the European Coal and Steel Community, designed to place those industries under supranational control and help tame the so-called national sinews of war. Like the New Deal, which influenced US postwar policy in Europe, American support for multilateral cooperation was set with an eye to the future. Institutionalised systems legitimising self-binding commitments helped deliver the stability that emerged. Although United States power at that stage was unmatched, it carried the responsibility of its limits. Global leadership was not by *diktat*, but by the marriage of material capacity to reciprocal obligations under international law.

The contrast with the present could not be more striking. Through prominent instances in recent years the United States has chosen to opt out of particular treaties, seek exemptions from proposed international regimes, or respond to global challenges alone. This includes rejection of the Comprehensive Test Ban Treaty; pursuit of a National Missile Defence and repudiation of the Anti-Ballistic Missile Treaty; repudiation of an original signature in support of the Rome Statute establishing the International Criminal Court; resistance to the optional verification protocol to the Biological Weapons Convention; refusal to accept inspections under the Chemical Weapons Convention; rejection of a proposed UN convention designed to curb the illicit traffic of small arms and light weapons; failure to sign the Ottawa Convention banning the production, trade and use of antipersonnel mines; reluctance to authorise or participate in UN peacekeeping operations (particularly in Africa); the withholding of annual dues and peacekeeping assessments to the UN; an imposition of external sanctions under the Helms-Burton Law; failure to ratify human rights treaties including Conventions on the Rights of the Child and the Elimination of Discrimination against Women; and repudiation of the Kyoto Protocol on global warming. In the Western hemisphere, the United States has not joined the 1994 Inter-American Convention for the Prevention, Punishment and Eradication of Violence against Women.

Within this culture of prickly exceptionalism three fields of current United States policy deserve brief comment. They concern the International Criminal Court, nuclear weapons proliferation, and development assistance.

United States opposition to the International Criminal Court stemmed in part from a refusal by the international community, when formulating the Rome Statute, to grant the United Nations Security Council control over the cases that the court considered and where the United States could exercise a veto if it wished. Instead, an independent prosecutor was favoured who, subject to safeguards and fair trial guarantees, would make such decisions. Determined to exempt US citizens or military abroad from the jurisdiction of the court, the United States concluded an array of bilateral deals to provide these individuals with immunity. The Bush administration in October 2003 even cut military aid to friendly countries refusing to accept such deals. This included states in Latin America and eastern and central Europe, presumably the first sanction in US diplomatic history targeted exclusively at democracies. Remarkably, Washington pressured Belgrade to sign the so-called Article 98 exemption clause while insisting that it surrender indicted war criminals to the War Crimes Tribunal in the Hague.

Washington also sought to obtain immunity for US nationals through the United Nations Security Council. In July 2002, under United States pressure, the council passed Resolution 1422 which seeks to give perpetual immunity from prosecution or investigation by the International Criminal Court to nationals of states that have not ratified the Rome Statute, but are involved in operations established or authorised by the United Nations. In June 2003 by a vote of twelve to nil (Syria, France and Germany abstaining) this provision was renewed for a further year. It is doubtful whether these resolutions conform to either the Rome Statute or the UN Charter. They exemplify the serious strains currently afflicting multilateralism. This is not whether the UN might survive without the political and financial support of the United States, but whether it can function effectively as a world organisation when its most powerful member launches a campaign designed to weaken one of its most significant recent initiatives.

What then of nuclear weapons proliferation? The United States Nuclear Posture Review of January 2002 indicates that nuclear weapons will remain part of the US military arsenal for at least the next fifty years. The idea is to plan attack options of the size required in order to pre-empt opposing threats, and supplement them through planning processes that are designed to anticipate a range of nuclear contingencies. The reduced total of operationally deployed warheads is not destroyed, just retired. Overall, and out to 2012, little actual disarmament is envisaged. The US Nuclear Posture Review speaks of a need for a revitalised nuclear weapons complex that is able if directed to design, manufacture and certify new warheads, and to maintain readiness to resume underground nuclear testing if required. The production of plutonium warheads has resumed.

These developments constitute a flat denial of the reciprocity that is clearly implicit in the joint agreement, reached at the 2000 Nuclear Non-Proliferation Treaty Review Conference, for an unequivocal undertaking to accomplish the total elimination of nuclear weapons. This outlined the practical steps needed to achieve that goal through the principles of transparency, verification and irreversibility.

To combat nuclear weapons proliferation, the United States has sought to alter legal standards regarding interdiction. With North Atlantic Treaty Organisation (NATO) countries, Australia and Japan, Washington has established what is termed the Proliferation Security Initiative. As of September 2003, this aimed to establish a coordinated approach for impeding or stopping shipments of weapons of mass destruction, delivery systems, and related materials flowing to and from states and non-state actors of proliferation concern.

Under Secretary Bolton stated, 'where we cannot convince a state to stop proliferant behaviour, or where items are shipped despite our best efforts to control them, we need the option of interdicting shipments to ensure the technology does not fall into the wrong hands. Properly planned and executed, interdicting critical weapons and technologies can help to prevent hostile states and terrorists from acquiring these dangerous capabilities.'[10]

Aimed primarily at North Korea, this initiative is designed to pressure that regime into cutting off exports of missile components or nuclear materials to other countries. Although a coalition of the willing, none of North Korea's land-bordering countries have agreed to join, while the arrangement has raised serious legal concerns regarding maritime interdiction in violation of rights of passage under the Law of the Sea Convention. Nothing in the Law of the Sea Convention explicitly prohibits transit of weapons of mass destruction or gives states rights to interdict such transit. Indeed, the United States with others has actively opposed the development of norms or interpretations of international law prohibiting such transit by seas or by air, citing that the rights and privileges established in the Law of the Sea affirm an unhindered military use of the oceans. However it is viewed, the Proliferation Security Initiative emerges as an example of the pursuit of United States national security interests via what is an opportunistic and *ad hoc* use or application of multilateral principles and processes

Development assistance

Since the attacks of September 2001 and the creation of a National Security Strategy designed to unite diplomacy, defence and development, the Bush administration has increasingly treated development assistance as a tool in its war against terrorism. This has seen enhanced reliance on private sector contractors, raised overall costs dramatically, and undercut efforts to lay the foundations for longer-term development as newly created delivery entities ignore the experience of long-standing US development assistance systems. This has resulted in the evanescent implementation of development assistance, limited transparency, inadequate consultation with recipients, and neglect of existing institutional experience. Focus on the war on terrorism has meant diverting attention from other needy regions, notably Africa and Latin America. Emphasis on short-term results tied to national security goals has imposed unrealistic indicators of success, and distorted the long-term development work necessary to produce sustainable reform and growth.[11]

These issues matter. A 2002 Pew Foundation survey, an exercise chaired by Madeleine Albright, about external attitudes to the US polled from a global cross section of some forty-four countries, found the commonest criticisms were that the US acts by itself, that it pushes policies widening the gap between rich and poor countries, and that it does not do enough to assist in solving the world's problems. The criticism that the US contributes to the gap between rich and poor countries was the negative sentiment that resonated most strongly among Americans with 39 per cent of survey respondents holding that view.[12]

Problems facing Washington's current policy on development assistance underline the systemic weaknesses afflicting the conduct of American multilateral diplomacy, its handling of UN Security Council affairs apart.

Too often American policy making here is improvised, haphazard and incoherent. The Bureau of International Organisation Affairs in the State Department has lost influence, while the foreign service offers no specialised career path in international organisational affairs. Reconstruction in Iraq I leave to others, except to say that Washington's policy has revealed failed processes of congressional deliberation, coordinated justification, and diplomatic reciprocity.[13]

Overall, the consequences of American unilateral exceptionalism will not abate quickly. This includes erosion of sovereign equality, which allows weaker states to enter into treaties with stronger countries on the assumption that such commitments are upheld. When that fabric of trust starts to weaken we enter a situation where the disparities of wealth and influence, already favouring the powerful in the formation of customary rules, grow even more entrenched.

Competing discourses

Following British nineteenth-century electoral reform, conducted in the interests of the middle class, Marx believed economics no longer was a question of whether 'this or that theorem was true but whether it was useful to capital or harmful, expedient or inexpedient, in accordance with police regulations or contrary to them'. Hence 'in place of the disinterested inquirers there stepped hired prize fighters; in place of genuine scientific research, the bad conscience and evil intent of the apologetic'.[14] Marx would probably have approved the term 'spin doctoring' that we now apply to these processes. For Russell Baker, 'among the privileges enjoyed by rich, superpower America is the power to invent public reality.'[15]

Yet however organised, discourse in the service of capital and production constitutes a force we cannot ignore—particularly given its formidable capacity to impose an assumed consensus between dominant and subordinate groups. Wealth creation for Maori in New Zealand for example, via forms of state asset redistribution or the market, is not divorced from this country's incorporation within global systems of production. We tempt fate, however, when we claim that the language explaining or justifying such processes is anything other than self-interested.

This centenary of George Orwell's birth reminds us of the significant role performed by language in serving the interests of those who determine foreign relations. Sometimes it operates as in-house code designed to rationalise the distribution of symbolic and material resources. This signifies understandings as to what is 'comfortable'; who is doing the 'heavy lifting', who is 'punching above their weight', or what is no more than 'a cigarette paper apart' in term of positions. In-house diplomatic code, however, can generate negativity by reinforcing differences between those who are 'in or out of the loop'. The fears of those left outside such connections can play to the advantage of others keen to play favourites for either group or bilateral purposes. By privileging sovereignty, this language does not challenge regime legitimacy, something evident for a lengthy period under Suharto's rule in Indonesia. For prominent Indonesian dissident author Pramoedya Toer the conditions that saw empty symbols, rhetoric and slogans employed to create a seeming 'reality' of the embryonic nation and state went unchallenged —an intellectual crisis of the mind that penetrated society.

The received language of diplomatic interaction thus conveys the bias of those at one within existing frameworks of order, blunter terminology dismissed as either shrill or unhelpful, or because it views such frameworks not as assisting solutions but contributing to problems.[16] Yet a more critical discursive approach does put the possibility of normative choices within current frameworks of social life increasingly in question. Where might these expanded horizons originate?

Russell Hardin detects what he terms street-level epistemology—a theory of knowledge drawn from the experiences of the ordinary person. John Gray believes liberal ideas are 'not embodiments of universal principles . . . but local understandings grounded in particular forms of common life'.[17] This differs from standard philosophical epistemology about justifying truth claims—or the criteria as to what makes claims true. Street-level epistemology offers a subjective account of knowledge. It has its own story to tell about how beliefs emerge—from religion, or from economic survival in the ghetto, *campesino* or refugee camp. This is utility knowledge following John Dewey's pragmatic rule that, in order to discover the meaning of an idea, we must ask about its consequences. Retention of office by fraud, those on the streets in Tbilisi recently concluded, carries implications of continuing poverty, unemployment and corruption. Those in Jakarta reasoned likewise in 1998.

Existing systems of information gathering have available a vast knowledge base linked to a huge social system and an immense division of labour. Yet the reliability of that knowledge system rests on extensive procedures of reciprocity. Defects here are less those of information overload or deficiency—though that can occur—than a lack of belief that ordinary knowledge from abroad has intrinsic worth distinct from the purposes for which it is sought. This entails intelligence less about position and capacity, than about implications and consequences. It requires the imagination needed to comprehend how ordinary people determine responses in reaction to the actions of outsiders. For all its technical sophistication, contemporary intelligence gathering in the service of much foreign and international security policy has not grasped the nature or significance of messages conveyed by the current street-level epistemologies driving the significant events of our time. That includes widely held beliefs among the globally dispossessed that the time has now arrived to hit back. That resentment will multiply unless multilateralism is able to represent the forces at work at the local as well as at the global level.

Implications for New Zealand

As a confirmed multilateralist, New Zealand's isolation has constantly reinforced its need to determine objectives against a cross section of external demands and interests. Aligning with first one state interest and then another, as occurred historically over some trade negotiations, this approach sought to cover as many bases as economically possible. That philosophy struck difficulty once alignment as insurance came into play—in particular the compartmentalisation of economic and security interests in ways that hid their interactions. Even with hindsight it was not difficult to forecast that, once the Americans began printing money rather than raising taxes to finance their deepening military immersion in Vietnam, trouble was gathering for New Zealand's future economic welfare as a global trader. Here, the insurance policies taken out with great and powerful friends could not deliver because the global consequences of the policies that they had unleashed proved beyond their control to manage.

These sobering events reinforced lessons taught following World War I, the Great Depression and World War II, namely that collective institutionalised endeavour, for all its faults, was not the best policy but the only policy. Peter Fraser at San Francisco glimpsed such an accommodation. In outline he championed an order advancing UN-supervised decolonisation, and the acceptance of the UN's planned Social and Economic Council as one of the principal UN organs. He also insisted that social and economic rights achieve a status comparable to those accorded civil and political rights.

Norman Kirk envisaged a structure of peaceful political, economic and social cooperation linking the Asia Pacific's uneasy state systems within a collaborative structure premised on the notion that peaceful relationships derived from equity. The goal of this accommodation remains unrealised, but its vision accords with the thesis of this chapter that New Zealand's foreign relations are least likely to lose focus so long as they maintain the impetus needed to achieve collaborative goals. New Zealand's antinuclear policy, rather than just iconic nationalism, makes most policy sense as a declaration of global collective responsibility—in particular through strategies designed to have nuclear weapons states meet their commitments to disarm.

In 1983, Prime Minister Muldoon warned in an article in *Foreign Affairs* about the likely costs of failing to exploit a period of global economic recovery to address structural issues of debt, protectionism, exchange-rate volatility, and needed macroeconomic coordination.[18] Some twenty years on—Muldoon's mixed legacy or limited progress on the reduction of agricultural subsidies aside—what has New Zealand achieved with others to effect such reforms? Results are limited, while existing structural arrangements facilitate capital flows that are replicating a grossly unequal world.

Having ventured down the road of deregulation, privatisation and capital mobility some critics view New Zealand as much a part of that problem as any component of a possible cure. The claim is that Branch Office New Zealand's national institutions, policies and practices adjust primarily not to public need but to the structures and dynamics of a world economy of capitalist production. I find this critique unduly reductionist, but its implications for democratic representation, not just in New Zealand but globally, remain serious. President Bush's Wilsonian enthusiasm for global democratisation, we might note, does not extend to the accountability and transparency of global finance.

Conclusions

Gradually but ineluctably, an appreciation has developed that, throughout its history, New Zealand has been hostage to its own good intentions willingly exploited by others. That risk of being used in the interests of major powers diminishes markedly once rule-based authorisations of commitment are entailed. Public opinion in New Zealand and elsewhere in 2003 was less hostile to the possible use of force against Iraq with, rather than without, formal UN authorisation. That response is emblematic of a view that deliberation conducted by multilateral means, effectively grounded in popular consent, offers widened choices for political action. We saw this over the Helsinki Process in Europe, the Ottawa Process leading to the landmines ban, and the World Court initiative on nuclear weapons. While not panaceas, and comprising numerous difficulties, these are workable modalities. The prescriptions for normative reciprocity that I have sketched require continuing attention to distributive equity and fairness. That remains the best answer to an illegal resort to force or the sound of shattering glass spreading from the streets of Seattle.

Notes

1   James L. Richardson, *Critical Liberalism in International Relations*, Working Paper 2002/7 (Canberra, Australian National University/RSPAS, 2002), p.12.
2   Andrew Hurrell, 'Security and Inequality' in Andrew Hurrell and Ngaire Woods (eds), *Inequality, Globalization, and World Politics* (Oxford, Oxford University Press, 1999), p.251.
3   Martha Finnemore, *National Interests in International Society* (Ithaca, NY, Cornell University Press, 1995), p.22.
4   Paul Kowert and Jeffrey W. Legro, 'Norms, Identity, and their Limits' in Peter J. Katzenstein (ed), *The Culture of National Security: Norms and Identity in World Politics* (Columbia, NY, Columbia University Press, 1996), pp.484–5.
5   For fuller development of this dichotomy, see Bruce Cronin, 'The Two Faces of the United Nations: The Tension between Intergovernmentalism and Transnationalism', *Global Governance*, 8, 1 (2002), pp.53–71.
6   Ngaire Woods, 'Holding Intergovernmental Institutions to Account', *Ethics and International Affairs*, 17, 1 (Spring 2003), p.69.
7   Woods, 'Holding Intergovernmental Institutions to Account', p.73.
8   Helen M. Simpson, *The Women of New Zealand* (Wellington, Department of Internal Affairs, 1940), p.185.
9   John G. Ruggie, 'Multilateralism: The Anatomy of an Institution' in John G Ruggie (ed), *Multilateralism Matters: The Theory and Praxis of an Institutional Form* (New York, Columbia University Press, 1993), p.25.
10 ' "Legitimacy" in International Affairs: The American Perspective in Theory and Operation'. Remarks of John R. Bolton, United States Under Secretary for Arms Control and International Security to the Federalist Society 13 November 2003, http://usinfo.state.gov/xarchives/display (30 November 2003), p.2.
11 For fuller discussion, see the November 2003 paper *Foreign Assistance in Focus: Emerging Trends* released by the major coalition of American non-governmental development assistance bodies (InterAction) and at http://www.interaction.org/files (20 November 2003), pp.1–15.
12 *What the World Thinks in 2002*, The Pew Research Center, December 2002, http://people-press.org/reports (18 November 2003), p.3.

13 Note the commentary by Thomas Powers claiming that the first round in the contest over Iraq policy occurred in the Senate Intelligence Committee where the majority drafted a critique that blamed the CIA, the minority arguing that deserving equal blame were marching orders emerging from the White House. 'The two sides could never agree but both were right. The administration could never have convinced Congress of its argument for war without the mystique of secret intelligence to impart gravity to its case; and the CIA would never have made so much of so little had George Tenet not been a willing member of the President's team. The problem was structural not personal.' Thomas Powers 'The Vanishing Case for War', *The New York Review of Books*, 50, 19 (4 December 2003), p.16.

14 Karl Marx, 'Afterword', *Capital, Volume 1* (London, Wishart, 1973), 2nd German edition, p.25.

15 Russell Baker, 'The Awful Truth', *The New York Review of Books*, 50, 17 (6 November 2003), p.5.

16 Robert Cox, 'Social Forces, States, and World Orders: Beyond International Relations Theory', *Millennium*, 10, 2 (1981), p.128.

17 John Gray, *Endgames: Questions in Modern Political Thought* (Cambridge, Polity Press, 1997), p.17.

18 Robert Muldoon, 'Rethinking the Ground Rules for an Open World Economy', *Foreign Affairs*, 61, 5 (Summer 1983), pp.1078–98.

NEW ZEALAND IN A GLOBALISING WORLD

2

DECONSTRUCTING GLOBALISATION

Alejandro Groppo[1]

In this chapter I develop a critique of the dominant discourse of globalisation. In order to do this the chapter will be structured into two sections. The first section introduces the main ideas underpinning the dominant idea of globalisation and the second develops an alternative view to this dominant discourse from the point of view of Latin America. This alternative view could also be seen as recognising the value and legitimacy of the developing world in general. In this analysis I maintain the hypothesis that the circulating idea of globalisation, among journalists, political, financial and economic elites, is just one view of a process that lacks precisely the characteristics of being 'global', being in the end a particular and a regional approach to world affairs. In other words, the dominant discourse of globalisation does not affirm that it is a multifarious process. Instead, it endorses the view that there are certain regularities tying different particular national and regional contexts. Contrary to the imagery of liberal-economic determinism, globalisation is neither ineluctable nor spontaneous and neutral. It has been the political project of an identifiable constellation of dominant interests that were, are and surely will be contestable and discussable.[2]

The dominant idea of globalisation

The discourse of globalisation emerges firstly from within the conceptual matrix of financial globalisation. This first understanding of globalisation *as* mainly a financial process still produces effects and it is a recurring image in the argumentative strategies of the 'pro-'globalisation positions. The original concept of globalisation was—even when this is already a reading of the process—a view of the economic and financial characteristics of the world. This discourse of financial-economic globalisation was supported and sustained in the last fifteen years by transnational corporations, global mass media and some metropolitan states. I call this powerful sector: the transnational historical bloc.

The historical origins of this discourse go back to the 60s and were reinforced by the economic crisis of the 70s, strengthened by the political failure of socialism of the 80s and the generalisation of the neoliberal paradigm in the 80s and 90s. It was in 1995, with the foundation of the World Trade Organisation (WTO), that the infrastructure of economic liberalisation and free trade were substantially strengthened and extended. The WTO wields unprecedented powers of surveillance and enforcement and has extended its ambit to include trade in services as well as trade-related investments and intellectual property issues.[3]

The WTO defends its mission by starkly contrasting a world of multilateral openness and market-led growth with one of closure and stagnation:

> the alternative to openness is protection against competition from imports and perpetual government subsidies. That leads to bloated inefficient companies supplying consumers with outdated unattractive products. Ultimately factories close and jobs are lost despite the production and subsidies. If other governments around the world pursue the same policies, markets contract and world economic activity is reduced. One of the objectives of the WTO is to prevent such a self-defeating and destructive drive into protectionism.[4]

Now, the powerful image of an open world without barriers is blatantly contradicted by the impossibility of any nature-based commodity coming from peripheral countries entering the central markets without high tariffs or import duties. What is at stake in the portrayal of globalisation-liberalisation as something 'positive' and protectionism as damaging is the power to define what is to be liberalised and free-traded and that power is concentrated upon the 'transnational historical bloc'. The laissez-faire fundamentalists did not only include international bankers or the technocratic elites of transnational organisations. President Clinton argued, along these lines, that while more open trade would have significant implications for the United States (US) economy, the political stakes were still higher:

> this new fabric of commerce will also shape the global prosperity or the lack of it, and with it the prospects of people around the world for democracy, freedom, and peace.[5]

It is interesting to show that globalisation as the expansion of free-market relations and economic liberalism is intrinsically attached to the attainment of political goals. This was bluntly clear in the case of the North American Free Trade Agreement (NAFTA) and the US and Mexico relationships. The dominant discourse affirmed that support for this project of regional integration had the important political consequences of ratifying, supporting and extending the market-oriented structural reforms of the Salinas regime. The support for NAFTA was also presented as support for the gradual reform of the Mexican political system and insinuated that all of this would help, by transitive implication, to extend promarket and prodemocracy reforms throughout the hemisphere, advancing the global agenda of a world system of multilateral openness. The dominant discourse of globalisation recognises that there is a 'political struggle not yet won', a goal to be striven towards through explicitly political strategies. Thus, while on the one hand the role of politics is made visible, on the other hand domestic goals are presented as purely economic. The logic of the overall process is justified in terms of its political gains while political discussion at home is delegitimised in the name of 'economic advantages'.

That the project of liberal globalisation (NAFTA was a paradigmatic example of this) has clear political stakes becomes evident when one examines the responses the project received at the domestic level. A group of twenty-five environmental and citizen activists denounced NAFTA as a scheme to enrich corporate capital at the expense of civic democratic representation:

> Promoted as a boon to all of us, the true purpose of NAFTA is to help large corporations increase their profits. NAFTA does this by undermining laws and standards that inhibit uncontrolled corporate activities. Freedom to circumvent democratically created environmental, health and safety laws. NAFTA will seriously stifle representative democracy by making local, state or national laws subjected to an unelected NAFTA bureaucracy that citizens cannot control.[6]

The resistance to the dominant view of the liberal global order highlights precisely its political horizon. This critique questions its political aims. In the view of the civic opposing groups, globalisation damages the democratic quality of political life by submitting political decisions to bureaucratic control. The deconstructive intervention against the hegemonic discourse of globalisation is a two-fold strategy. On the one hand, deconstruction implies a critique from outside which highlights different political aims as announced by social activists antagonistic to the globalisation process. The contest over the political meaning of the process of globalisation represents a decentring of the political aims of the dominant groups. To contest those political aims (globalisation equals democracy and peace) is to make visible the blatant arbitrariness of that isomorphism and to induce people to believe that things could also be otherwise (that globalisation could also mean international inequality and, in the end, war).

On the other hand, a deconstructive strategy towards the discourse of globalisation would assume the form of an internal critique. This second avenue to the inner core of the discourse of globalisation is quite different from the first strategy described above. The following section is devoted to its analysis.

Globalising 'globalisation'

An internal deconstruction of the dominant ideology supporting the hegemonic view of globalisation means an expansion of its literal content. In other words, through an assumption of the 'global' character of our contemporary world, this strategy intends to show that the idea of 'globalisation' underpinning the dominant order is a restricted one; it is just a particular, regional view of the world that is Eurocentric in character and aims to expand its own interests by erasing differences and eliminating otherness. A real idea of 'globality' or an authentic view of the 'global' necessarily includes the opposing idea of the 'local'. The global implies the local as its underside. A 'global' that excludes the 'local' or any 'local' is not a real global but another 'local', it is a restricted global, a particular and regional global. By characterising the local as 'primitive', 'a return to the past' or a 'persistence of barbarism and oscurantism', the idea of globalisation produced in the centres shows precisely its lack of universality.

Let me now analyse in more depth this prevailing exclusionary logic within the discourse of globalisation. The discourse of (economic, financial, free-market) globalisation is structured on the dream of a non-divided humanity. It seems to be grounded in an idea of a 'global community' without heals and rifts. The dominant idea of globalisation draws, in the last instance, upon the sources of the millenarian fantasy of global harmony. Together with this core idea other adjacent issues come to the fore, i.e. that globalisation is some kind of abstract universality, that globalised economic relations are supplanting familiar social relations, cultural identities and political forms.[7]

The problem with this view of a seamless global world is that it cannot prevent the production of alternative views. Among the most important alternative perspectives that emerged within the paradigm of globalisation were those within the rich area of postcolonial and subaltern studies produced in academic and non-governmental centres in Latin American and US universities. The fields of critical cultural studies and comparative literature have been fertile producers of works discussing the Eurocentric and colonial implications behind the dominant view of globalisation.[8]

Fernando Coronil, for example, affirms that a critical analysis of present views of globalisation must necessarily include a critical and more comprehensive view of capitalism.[9] Capitalism, in Coronil's view, cannot be understood only from the binary formula 'capital'–'labour'. As a generalised organising system, it needs to be understood through the incorporation of a third element: nature or land. If 'nature' is included as an important element in the discussion of capitalism, then this system cannot be interpreted any more as an essentially European construction. The incorporation of 'nature' in the critical discourse of capitalism plays a double role. Firstly, it makes room for the incorporation of those peoples and institutions that depend upon the mercantilisation of the so-called 'intensive-nature commodities'. Secondly, it puts forward the challenging idea that nature implies a type of universalisation that does not exclude differences. As Coronil affirms:

> To integrate 'land' into the 'capital-labour' relationship helps us to understand the processes that constituted the mutual formation of Europe and its colonies. Instead of a narrative of history structured upon an opposition between a modern Europe that succeeded on the basis of its own efforts, and a periphery plunged into backwardness, this change of perspective allows us to appreciate the [neo] colonial nature of the relation between metropolitan modernity and the subaltern.[10]

In the view proposed by those studies, the worldwide opening of the perception of capitalism has a theoretically strategic aim: to emphasise and recover in a way the originary relation that capitalism had with colonialism. In this view it displaces the understanding of capitalism as a purely particular phenomenon and starts thinking of it in 'global' terms. It also contributes by describing the global dynamics in terms of violence and not in terms of modernisation.

Thus, the contribution of subaltern studies to the analysis of globalisation has an extraordinary outcome: it challenges the idea of a 'unique' and one-way road to a globalised world showing that the very discourse of globalisation is in itself perspectival.

To recognise the essential perspectival character of political language (of which the language of globalisation is just an example) is the first step to a more tolerant, plural and open mode of thinking. The dominant discourse of globalisation remained blind to a wide variety of aspects of current world affairs. The 1997 United Nations Conference on Trade and Development Report stated six main problems of the contemporary global economy:

1. the level of growth of the world economy was lower than was expected
2. there was an increasing gap between poor and rich countries. The international inequality was correlative with an increasing gap within developed and developing counties. Thus, a new era of social justice was required at the global and national level. For example: in 1965 the gross domestic product per person of the richest 20 per cent of nations was thirty times higher than that of the poorest 20 per cent, while in 1999 that gap was seventy times greater
3. within the countries, the wealthiest sectors won in relation not only to poor sectors but also to the middle sectors
4. the finance sector had benefited over the industrial sector and the rentiers over the investors
5. participation of capital in the global income had increased more than labour participation
6. there was an increasing gap between specialised and non-specialised labour.

An important issue challenges us now: is our analysis not about the recognition of the deconstructive role of 'place', 'nature' and 'land'? Is this not another way of essentialising, feminising, or dehistorising these roles? Does this not mean falling back into the mistakes we are trying to overcome? Is not the recovery of the 'local' as a 'marginalised' place another way of reconstituting the discourse of globalisation as modernisation and space?[11] The answer in every case is no.

Conclusions: Rethinking the local and the global

Throughout this chapter I have displaced the discussion of globalisation towards its margins. Those margins should be understood literally: the new political economy of post-development is pressing for an incorporation of the regions excluded from the economic centres. Latin America is one of them. The new ways of thinking are coming from post-structuralism, political ecology and critical anthropology and have been affirming the critical role of the 'local' as an alternative to a view blindly centred in the 'global' as a capitalist and European global. But this reaffirmation of the 'local' is not without challenges. A variety of new questions emerge with these issues: what notions of 'democracy', 'politics', 'development' and 'economy' are needed to reinforce the effectiveness of the local, with all its richness and contradictions? What role do the new social actors need to play in order to create networks to support the multifarious local forms of life that could offer alternatives to the sometimes alienating and superfluous forms of life prevalent in our globalised world?

Notes

1 Lecturer in Political Theory at the National University of Villa Maria, Argentina. alegroppo@hotmail.com.
2 Among others, important critics of the transnationalised economy are: Paul Hirst, G. Thompson, L Sklair. 'A problematisation of the globalising process' in P. Hirst and G. Thompson, *Globalisation in Question* (Cambridge, Polity Press, 1996).
3 M. Rupert, *Ideologies of Globalisation: Contending visions of the new world order* (London, Routledge, 2000), p.45.
4 World Trade Organisation, *Trading into the Future* (Geneva, WTO, 1998), 2nd edition, p.8.
5 W. J. Clinton, 'Address to the World Trade Organisation' (Geneva, US Mission, 1999).
6 Quoted in L. Wallach, 'Hidden Dangers of GATT and NAFTA' in R. Nader (ed), *The Case against Free Trade* (San Francisco, Earth Island Press, 1993), p.43.
7 See A. Dirlik, 'Place-based Imagination: Globalism and the politics of place' in Arif Dirlik (ed), *Place and Politics in the Age of Global Capitalsim* (New York, Rowman and Littlefield, 2000).
8 An interesting work highlighting the political implications of critical cultural theory from a Latin American perspective is J. Beverly, *Subalternity and Representation: Arguments in Cultural Theory* (Durham, NC, Duke University Press, 1999).
9 Coronil, F. 'Naturaleza del Poscolonialismo: del eurocentrismo al globocentrismo' in E. Lander (ed), *La Colonialidad del Saber: eurocentrismo y ciencias sociales* (Buenos Aires, Clacso, 2000).
10 Coronil, 'Naturaleza del Poscolonialismo: del eurocentrismo al globocentrismo' p.92.

11 The difference between space and place is brightly established by Arturo Escobar in 'El Lugar de la naturaleza y la naturaleza del lugar: globalización o postdesarrollo?' in E. Lander (ed), *La Colonialidad del Saber: eurocentrismo y ciencias sociales.*

3

THE MARSDEN 'GLOBALISATION AND NEW ZEALAND' PROJECT

Brian Easton

In late 2003 I was awarded a three-year Marsden Grant to study globalisation and New Zealand's role in it. This chapter sketches the research programme, which is primarily driven from an economist's perspective, but also poses some of the international relations issues.

It is a topic I have been long working upon, developing out of my earlier study of the New Zealand economy summarised in my book *In Stormy Seas: The Post-War New Zealand Economy*. The book's theme is that the fate of New Zealand will be largely a consequence both of what happens overseas, and our ability to seize the opportunities and manage the problems those events prevent.

The topic creates definitional problems. Many writers avoid defining globalisation analytically, instead characterising it by a series of particular phenomena such as increasing trade, or capital flows, or logos, or international inequality; or by relating it to particular international institutions such as the World Trade Organisation (WTO) or the International Monetary Fund (IMF) and the World Bank or the European Union, or multinational corporations. Alternatively they highlight particular policies such as free trade, liberalised capital movements, and so on. The London *Economist* described globalisation as 'international capitalism': many antiglobalisers might agree, perhaps adding 'together with US [United States] hegemony' or even 'imperialism'.

Stanley Fischer, one time chief economist at the IMF, describes globalisation as 'the ongoing process of greater interdependence among countries and their citizens'.[1] Joseph Stiglitz, who held a similar position at the World Bank, defines globalisation as 'the closer integration of countries of the world as a result of lowering transportation and communication costs, and the removal of artificial man-made barriers'.[2] Both are focused on contemporary phenomena. But it is important that we take a historical perspective. Scholars argue that nineteenth-century globalisation was in many ways a more powerful and pervasive phenomenon than that of the late twentieth century, at least among peoples of European origin, because migration was unrestricted.

Moreover, it was not just an internation phenomenon. Indeed it would be ahistoric to think of the states of the beginning of the nineteenth century as similar to those of today. The modern nation-state was a creation of the globalisation process of the times, as it integrated regions and made central government and national markets possible. The 'United' States of America became a more meaningful concept when canals and railways brought the federation of states geographically closer together.

In the end a simple phenomenon-based definition like Fischer's, may be the most fruitful. We follow Stiglitz, albeit also covering the nineteenth century, with *globalisation as the closer integration of nations and regions.*

However, for an economist, a definition is not sufficient. We need a process, a mechanism which underpins the phenomenon. The research programme is organised around the analytical proposition of *globalisation as the consequences of the reductions in the costs of distance.*

That these falls have been dramatic is easily demonstrated by considering the world centred on New Zealand. One hundred and fifty years ago it took three months to sail from Britain to New Zealand—carrying goods, people and information. Changes since then have reduced the shipping time to about three weeks, quartering the effective distance in the world. But people, and light valuable goods can fly to Britain in under two days, a reduction of about 98 per cent. Information can be zipped around the world virtually instantaneously.

If these changes are not spectacular enough, think of the changes for meat and dairy products. One hundred and fifty years ago, one could not ship them to Britain at all. The introduction of refrigeration reduced the cost of distance from (effectively) infinity, to a small proportion of the products' costs of production, and transformed New Zealand's economy and society.

There is another lesson here. The cost of distance does not diminish uniformly for all products, people and information. Therein lies its problem, although the technical explanation for it belongs to another discussion. Even so, a short sketch of the economic analytics may be helpful.

In some useful ways, the costs of distance are analogous to tariffs. The theory of tariffs tells us that while a total elimination of tariffs can be beneficial—in a certain limited sense, under certain restrictive assumptions—a partial reduction may not. The best-known example is that a partial free-trade agreement need not be beneficial to the participants, if the trade diversion effects are greater than the trade creation effects. Analogously a reduction in the costs of distance (which is always partial) may not be of benefit in all destinations. Much of regional policy is predicated on this outcome, but it can apply also to countries. The regional example also highlights a resolution: if everyone is sufficiently mobile then those in the depressed region can migrate to the prospering one. But in practice not all the population can easily move and the differential labour mobility can compound the region's difficulties. The same applies between countries, with the additional complication that (nineteenth-century Europeans excepted) there are severe restrictions on labour mobility. The implication is that a reduction in the costs of distance, and the consequent increased globalisation, need not be beneficial to all the countries and regions affected.

Of course, very often it is, but there is a tendency to accept the beneficial upside of any change and grumble about the detrimental downsides. This effect is reinforced by another result, evident in trade theory but which arises much more widely. A technological change can alter the income distribution, and make some people worse off. In the case of a fall in the cost of distance, it is not only that the increase in air travel has been a set back for sailors (that is, an industry effect) but that industries may leave regions with consequent loss of wages to its workers (that is, a location effect). Thus there is a considerable political backlash against globalisation, which reflects some of the damage that the process generates for particular workers and regions, albeit without an understanding of the entirety of the process, good and bad.

Another complication is that, as trade theory shows, economies of scale—in the production process or in an industry—undermine some of the clarity of even the limited conclusions of traditional trade theory. But the recent developments involving economies of scale and differentiated product also enhance its relevance to the real world.

In particular an important postwar phenomenon has been the rise of intra-industry trade, where broadly the same product is exchanged between different countries (Germans may buy Renaults and the French Volkswagens). Intra-industry trade hardly existed fifty years ago, but today it makes up about a quarter of the world's trade, and so is one of the fastest growing parts of it. It cannot be explained merely by comparative advantage—the underpinning notion in traditional trade theory. The relevant concept to describe the new phenomenon is 'competitive advantage', although of course a phrase cannot capture all the subtleties of the analysis.

New Zealand has a low involvement in intra-industry trade. Among the industrial nations it is near the bottom (on some measures Australia is a little lower), more like a developing country than a rich one. Undoubtedly comparative advantage served New Zealand well in the past (and undoubtedly we should continue to enhance it by seeking reductions in international barriers to primary product trade). But it seems likely that for long-term survival the economy needs to accelerate its intra-industry trade—shifting to a better balance: from comparative advantage to competitive advantage. In my view that is much of what the government's Growth and Innovation Strategy is about: for the vision implicitly has New Zealand exporting pharmaceuticals to Europe, information technology to the US and films to Hollywood, as well as importing drugs from Europe, IT from the US and films from Hollywood. The strategy's difficulty is that competitive advantage involves different policies from those appropriate for comparative advantage. (This is in addition to the challenge of creating new competitive advantage industries in an environment where many of the established comparative advantage industries remain successful.) We are only learning what those better policies might be.

Not surprisingly, given my disciplinary training, the Marsden's research programme is founded on the economics of globalisation. However, there are some wider issues, which I hope to look at if there is time.

One is the impact of globalisation on culture. There is the possibility of 'convergence'—where the forces of globalisation eliminate cultural differences—or independence—where some choice of national living style is possible. I am alternately optimistic and pessimistic about this outcome—even in the same paragraph. I am going through a mildly optimistic phase at the moment, after observing that despite more than one hundred years of strong globalisation, the United States still contains a number of vigorous cultures within its melting pot, while Canadians are distinct from Americans in numerous ways, despite their closeness to the US and the degree of economic integration between the two economies. This is not to deny that globalisation has, and will, profoundly affect the course of cultural development, and it seems likely that it will extinguish some cultures or meld them into others. The difficulty—as in most things to do with globalisation—is in identifying changes which would have happened anyway and not being deceived by a reluctance to let go of the past.

A particularly interesting element of culture is the diaspora, those that live outside the geographical boundaries of a culture (or where, in effect, there are no boundaries, as applied to the Jews for more than a millennium). Because diasporas are, in part, the consequences of labour mobility, they are an integral part of the Marsden project.

A variation on the cultural issue, although also with significant other facets ranging from economics to international relations, is the changing role of the nation-state. In many ways nation-states are the creation of nineteenth-century globalisation. I expect to pay particular attention to the history of Germany, a nation-state created in the nineteenth century (it is said that it is the consequence of railways). And yet the same globalisation processes, initially working through the European Union (EU), may change the state out of recognition by the end of the twenty-first century. Intriguingly German culture is at least 500 years old, and may outlast the German state.

Nostalgia aside, the changing role of the nation-state is arguably the consequence of a need to impose a common rule of economic law in international intercourse, just as the rise of the nation-state in the nineteenth century was in part necessary to create regional economic order. (Think of the Zollverein, the customs union which contributed to the establishment of Germany.) Similarly, increased international, economic intercourse is leading to supranational organisations such as the WTO. They are a consequence of globalisation not its drivers. (There may be a similar phenomenon, that is, institution creation in the international political order.) Those who grumble about supranational institutions often miss the point, which is not their existence but how they function. A useful parallel is how national governments initially acted in the interests of the elite, but how over time they became more democratic and act more in the interests of all. I would have thought the grumblers should be more concerned with the democratisation of the supranational organisations rather than the elimination which their rhetoric often conveys.

Indeed, one might draw a parallel with today's antiglobalisers and their nineteenth-century predecessors, who were concerned with the effects of industrialisation (in part a consequence of the globalisation of the day) and saw that industrialisation was destructive for people and the communities they lived in. The resistors of the day identified the hardship, but they took two broadly different approaches to it. There were those, such as Pierre-Joseph Proudhon, who wanted to reverse the process and return to some sort of (as it happens) idealised past. But the English radical tradition wanted to harness industry for the benefit of society. Today we live a far more comfortable life than our nineteenth-century ancestors because they succeeded. (Karl Marx went further and saw industrialisation as a process which was inherently progressive and would lead to benefits for the workers. He may have been correct, although the actual path was different from that which he vaguely predicted and some of his followers attempted to enforce.)

The implication of this is that the supranational organisations which the antiglobalisers detest are not so much wrong institutions, but flawed institutions which need to be democratised (although what exactly democracy means in this context has to be clarified). The optimist may expect this to happen in due course: the realist may expect a lot of hardship on the way.

It is not obvious that the creation of supranational organisations effectively eliminates nation-states. Some interesting analysis by economists Alberto Alesina and Enrico Spolaore argues that middle-sized nations (that would include New Zealand) perform economically more effectively than larger ones.[3] While there may be economies of size in some economic production processes which benefit large nations' economies, they seem to be offset by diseconomies of governance. Large nations have difficulty managing the diversities in their population, while smaller economies offset their economic size disadvantage through international trade. The counter-example is the US, which is both large and economically very successful. The authors argue that the US is organised in a very decentralised way, with the implication being that in order to survive as effective nation-states, it is necessary that the governance be as decentralised as practicable. If that is true for nations, it may also be true for the world as a whole. A natural unit of decentralisation—but not the only one—is the nation-state, which suggests there may be a role for nation-states in a highly globalised world albeit, no doubt, a different one from that of today.

Moreover, Alesina and Spolaore point out that the existing international boundaries are not inviolate. Indeed there are more than three times as many countries as there were fifty years ago. While this might be seen as a process of decolonisation, the break up of the Soviet Union is an example of what may be better described as democratisation, which might be the ideal of decolonisation.

This analysis, which its authors extend in a number of different directions, is undoubtedly attractive, but it ignores the fact that whatever the strength of markets as a way of resolving people's needs, they exist in a context of rules and that different rules give different market outcomes. Size and military power may be important in determining how much influence a country has on defining those rules, and inevitably each will attempt to influence the rules in their own interests. The implication is that globalisation may begin with the economic phenomenon of reducing costs of distance—and there is much economic analysis to follow—but a comprehensive approach requires political and social (and cultural analysis too). Whether the Marsden project (or its researcher) has the resources to tackle these non-economic questions is a matter to be addressed in the future. At the very least it should provide a foundation for others to tackle them.

Even the limited economic focus reminds us that size is not necessarily a disadvantage, providing the economy is reasonably open. Thus it is not only ahistorical to bemoan New Zealand's size—in the past the economy was more affluent relative to the rest of the world despite being relatively smaller—but the pessimism is not consistent with current economic analysis. Similarly it is ahistorical to bemoan distance as a major problem for New Zealand's economic growth—the economy was practically further from the rest of the world in the nineteenth century, but that did not prevent solid economic growth—and it ignores the fact that distance is diminishing for practical economic intercourse.

Such thinking leads to defeatism, since it suggests there is little option but to grow slowly. (Merging with Australia is sometimes associated with these attitudes, but an Australasian economy would still be small and distant on a world scale.) Instead the evidence says that while size and distance are problems for New Zealand, they also present opportunities.

Just what those opportunities are, is what the Marsden project is about. However, the core of the project is to understand the phenomenon of globalisation, not to judge it, and certainly not to come to definitive policy conclusions. By sharing the understandings of globalisation that the funding enables me to pursue, I hope that my Marsden research project will help New Zealand, and the world, to learn to cope better with, and to better control, one of the most powerful processes shaping the future.

Notes

1   Stanley Fischer, 'Globalisation and Its Challenges', *AEA Papers and Proceedings: American Economic Review*, 93, 2 (2003), pp.1–30.
2   Joseph Stiglitz, *Globalization and Its Discontents* (New York, W.W. Norton, 2002).
3   Alberto Alesina and Enrico Spolaore, *The Size of Nations* (Cambridge, MIT Press, 2003).

4

SOVEREIGNTY, GLOBALISATION AND NEW ZEALAND FOREIGN POLICY

Robert Patman

Structural changes in the global system have raised a big question mark over a traditional working principle of international relations, namely, state sovereignty. With the end of the Cold War and the subsequent break up of the Soviet Union in 1991, the United States (US) has been left as the world's only superpower. As a result, the relative power of the US in the new international hierachy has sharply increased, a trend that has prompted some observers to characterise the post-Cold War system as unipolar. At the same time, the post-Cold War world has been subject to deepening globalisation, a process that is associated with the growth of international linkages and a reduction in the capacity of nation-states to act independently. Such radical changes in the international landscape, according to a former United Nations secretary general, Boutros Boutros Ghali, meant that the 'time of absolute and exclusive national sovereignty has passed'.[1] But has there ever been a time when states have exercised absolute and exclusive sovereignty?

This chapter will analyse the impact of a changing world on the foreign policy of New Zealand and in particular to what extent globalisation has affected the sovereign capacity of New Zealand to act upon the international stage? With this in mind, the chapter proceeds in five stages. First, it attempts to delineate the concepts of sovereignty and globalisation. Second, it examines three competing schools of thought in the sovereignty-globalisation debate. Third, it considers the domestic dimension to New Zealand's foreign policy. Fourth, it identifies some patterns in the evolution of New Zealand's foreign policy. Finally it evaluates the impact of globalisation over the last two decades, in terms of New Zealand's national identity, economic diplomacy, security concerns and multilateral commitments.

The basic argument that emerges is that while New Zealand has been profoundly affected by the process of globalisation, this has not necessarily involved a substantial erosion of state sovereignty. In fact, by challenging traditional symbols of power in the international system, such as geography and size, globalisation has created new possibilities for New Zealand to promote its core values and interests externally.

Conceptualising sovereignty and globalisation

Sovereignty has often been regarded as the enabling concept of international relations. The Treaty of Westphalia in 1648 marked the beginning of the contemporary doctrine of state sovereignty. This concept has internal and external dimensions, although the two may coexist to different degrees.[2] Max Weber said a sovereign state was 'an institution claiming to exercise a monopoly of legitimate force within a particular territory'.[3] In other words, a sovereign state is one that exercises supreme, legal, unqualified and exclusive control over a designated territory and its population. At the same time, the sovereignty of a state requires recognition by other states through diplomatic relations and usually by membership of a comprehensive international organisation like the United Nations (UN). The doctrine of sovereignty is based on the notion of formal equality between states and the principle of non-intervention in matters that are essentially seen as domestic affairs of a state.

It should be added that there are close to 200 sovereign states at the beginning of the twenty-first century and they vary greatly in territorial size, natural resources, governing capacity and function, military capability, economic strength, size of population and so forth. Paradoxically, the doctrine of state sovereignty reinforces the notion of international anarchy: the idea of a supreme authority within the state logically leads to a denial of the existence of a suprasovereign above the state, except in those instances where the state explicitly confers authority on an international organisation.

In comparison to sovereignty, globalisation is a much more difficult concept to precisely define, despite a vast literature on the subject. Globalisation is a process rather than an ideology or a programme. It may be broadly defined as the rising intensity of interconnections between societies, institutions, cultures, and individuals on a worldwide basis. Globalisation implies 'a shift in geography' whereby borders have become increasingly porous.[4] That is to say, the process of globalisation involves a compression of time and space, shrinking distances through a dramatic reduction in the time taken, either physically or representationally, to cross them. As a result, the world seems a smaller place as issues of the environment, economics, politics and security intersect more deeply at more points.[5] This pattern has arguably been underway for more than a century. But it gained real momentum durings the 1980s when technologically driven revolutions in communications and production, and related developments like trade liberalisation, massive financial transactions and global mass media networks served to promote the idea of a 'common consciousness' of human society 'on a world scale'.[6]

Yet globalisation is not simply a homogenising process that necessarily subordinates local or national concerns to broader ones. On the contrary, the effects of enhanced connections across borders can be profoundly uneven. This process can entrench existing patterns of inequality and hierarchy in the international arena or actually fuel new ethnic, religious conflicts and economic divisions.[7] To date, the post-Cold War world seems to have been caught between the opposing trends of integration and fragmentation—trends that are closely associated with the impact of globalisation.

The sovereignty-globalisation debate

The interaction between the concept of state sovereignty and the process of globalisation has generated a lively debate. Theoretically, there appears to be a certain tension between the two elements. The primacy of the state-centric international structure appears to be increasingly challenged by the fact that globalisation has helped to spawn a multicentric world of transnational actors ranging from multinational corporations to terrorist groups. The proliferation of these non-state actors would seem directly or indirectly to affect the capacity of the sovereign state to serve as a single and autonomous political authority within a territory. Furthermore, because globalisation is making the world a smaller place, the pressures for regulating the international arena with new rules of behaviour are increasing.[8] But the extension of the rule of law would serve to moderate the anarchy of the international arena and thus encroach on the ability of the sovereign state to act externally in an authoritative fashion.

If we concede the possibility of a connection between sovereignty and globalisation, a major issue remains: what is the precise nature of this relationship? Three major schools of thought have emerged on this issue. First, there is one known as the hyperglobalist approach. According to this perspective, the growing interconnectedness of national economies through globalisation negates the significance of territorial boundaries and paves the way for the demise of the sovereign nation-state.[9] The hyperglobalists contend that one of the crucial effects of globalisation has been to reduce the space for states to manage national macroeconomic policy. With the creation of a single global market, it is argued that globalisation effectively denationalises the economies of sovereign states through the establishment of transnational networks of production, trade and finance. In this borderless economy, national governments are said to have little option but to sustain a policy mix that is consistent with the requirements of global capital and international competitiveness. The underlying thesis here is that the rise of multinational corporations as international actors and the emergence of new mechanisms for global governance such as the World Trade Organisation (WTO) are symptomatic of a new world order in which the sovereign state is becoming marginalised.[10] Such a perspective, however, seems to assume that the notion of state sovereignty is a static one and that the effects of globalisation are experienced evenly by all states.

Second, another school of thought has been called the sceptics. The sceptics believe that little has changed in the international arena. Rejecting the hypoglobalist position as politically naïve, the sceptics argue that the impact of globalisation on the sovereign state is much exaggerated. In this view, the state is not the victim of this process, but its main architect.[11] Sceptics emphasise that sovereign states play a central role in the regulation and active promotion of cross-border economic links. Key state actors such as the US are said to have played a leadership role in spearheading the globalisation process. Washington and other like-minded states, for example, continue to negotiate the global regulation of multilateral trade agreements and have driven the emergence of supranational organisations like the WTO.[12] The sovereign state is also deemed to be the sole institution tasked with the responsibility for establishing the preconditions for economic activity: political stability, the rule of law, education and training, and infrastructure are among the elements that play a part here.[13] As a consequence, it is argued that transnational players like multinational corporations need capable states and a stable state system to function successfully. Indeed, many multinational corporations remain largely 'nationally embedded' and still look to sovereign states for regulating their activities through policies and rules.[14] So the sceptics maintain the sovereignty of the state has not been substantially diminished by globalisation. Such a view, however, rests on the conviction that contemporary levels of interconnectedness are not unprecedented, and sovereign states retain as much power internationally as they had in the past.

The third school of thought is a middle ground position between the hyperglobists and sceptics. It has been labelled the transformationalist view. It rejects the tendency to juxtapose state sovereignty and globalisation. According to this perspective, the state should not be seen as being diminished by globalisation nor unaffected by it. Rather, the role of the sovereign state in the international system is being redefined by globalisation because states themselves recognise that the power, authority, and functions of government must be transformed in response to the growing interconnectedness of the world.[15] This school argues sovereignty is a dynamic concept that, since its introduction, has evolved from a royal form into a more popular manifestation. In Barkin's words, 'sovereignty has never been absolute. States have never been able to do what they want.'[16] Thus, sovereignty in conditions of globalisation is undergoing a new phase in its evolution. Viewed in this way, the increase of multilateral agreements in the period of globalisation does not symbolise the decline of state sovereignty. More often than not, states choose to enter into multilateral arrangements because they pragmatically recognise they are increasingly confronted by 'problems without passports' that cannot be solved on a national basis. The transformation of the sovereign state during globalisation, however, is qualified by the inequalities of power in the international system. The transformationalist perspective tends to assume that globalisation has an equal impact on all sovereign states.

How does New Zealand fit into this debate on the relationship between sovereignty and globalisation? What has been the impact of globalisation on New Zealand's foreign policy? Has it reflected a steady leakage of New Zealand sovereignty to supranational groups? Or has New Zealand's foreign policy continued to be largely shaped by the competitive system of sovereign states? Alternatively, has globalisation generated a new foreign policy by transforming the nature of the sovereign state in New Zealand?

New Zealand's domestic environment

A starting point for understanding New Zealand's foreign policy during the last two decades is its domestic environment. Major features include its small size, democratic political system, and unique national attributes. The international relations literature suggests that two of the typical characteristics of small states are an internationalist orientation, consisting of keen participation in international and regional organisations, and a moral emphasis in external policy.[17] External organisations offer states with limited resources the opportunity to maximise their diplomatic efforts on the international stage. They also help to uphold international rules and norms that protect weak states from potential interference by more powerful ones.

New Zealand is a democratic society that is based on political and legal traditions derived from the Westminister parliamentary model of governance. The intimacy and transparency of the New Zealand political system means that public opinion is potentially a far more potent factor in the shaping of foreign policy than is normally the case in larger countries. Nevertheless, while public engagement in foreign policy has grown markedly since the 1960s, it remains subject to an important qualification: despite being elected members of parliament, cabinet ministers remain extraordinarily dependent on the advice of their bureaucratic advisors, in this case the Ministry of Foreign Affairs and Trade (MFAT).[18] Although organisations such as the New Zealand Institute of International Affairs (NZIIA), the Centre for Strategic Studies (CSS) in Wellington and the annual University of Otago Foreign Policy School have advanced the level of discussion on foreign policy, they are too small and few in number to seriously contest MFAT's dominance as the main source of advice for government on foreign affairs. MFAT officials provide ministers with institutional memory of prior policies adopted, modified and supplanted. They interpret New Zealand's overseas obligations under treaties, international law and precedents and, through ministers, they research and present policy alternatives from which the cabinet may make its decisions. At the same time, polling evidence indicates that the New Zealand public remains much less focused on foreign than on domestic policy.[19]

New Zealand manifests some, though by no means all, of the characteristics commonly associated with a small state. Although it has a small gross domestic product (GDP) and only modest military capabilities, when viewed in the regional context of the South Pacific, New Zealand appears to be a relatively significant power.[20] As well as retaining the status of an administrative trustee power, and having constitutional responsibilities towards the Cook Islands, Niue and Tokelau, New Zealand is unique for its geographical isolation and absence of any direct security threat in the post-Cold War era. That situation is not typical for many states and has given Wellington some freedom of manoeuvre on a range of international issues.

The evolution of New Zealand foreign policy

The emergence of a distinctive New Zealand foreign policy is a fairly recent development. From 1769, when Captain Cook first sighted the east coast of the North Island, until the end of the Second World War, New Zealand's status as a British colony meant that foreign policy was largely defined in London. While it had established its own diplomatic corps and military forces by the late 1930s, it still saw itself as one of Britain's staunchest allies. However, the pattern of New Zealand's external relations significantly changed after 1945. Australia gradually replaced Britain as New Zealand's major bilateral partner. Several factors played a part in this. First, there was a cumulative realisation in Wellington and Canberra that Britain was no longer in a position to defend them militarily. Doubts had begun with the British defeat at Singapore in February 1942.[21] In 1944, the two countries signed their first major solely bilateral agreement without Britain when they concluded a mutual defence pact in Canberra, often known as the ANZAC (Australia and New Zealand Army Corps) Treaty.[22] The Canberra Pact provided for cooperation in the South Pacific and was progressively expanded as the two allies fought together in wars in Korea, Malaysia and Vietnam.

Second, the international pressures associated with the Cold War after 1947 propelled both New Zealand and Australia into a strategic alignment with the United States. In 1951, Australia, New Zealand and the United States signed the ANZUS Treaty. This was basically a trilateral collective security agreement. Over the next thirty years, the US displaced Britain as the principal strategic partner of the ANZAC countries as the former colonial power retreated to Europe following the Suez Crisis of 1956 and the 1968 decision to withdraw the British navy from stations 'East of Suez'.[23] Australia and New Zealand subsequently participated in the UN-sanctioned but US-led intervention on behalf of South Korea against the attack from North Korea in 1950–53. Both supported the defence of Western interests under the leadership of the US through the ANZUS Treaty and the South East Asia Treaty Organisation (SEATO). Both also assisted Britain in its defence of Malaysia against Indonesia in 1963–65; and sent troops to fight alongside the US in its unsuccessful bid to save South Vietnam from communism in 1964–75.[24]

Third, New Zealand and Australia had to deal with the consequences of Britain joining the European Union (EU) (then the European Economic Community–EEC) in January 1973. This development had been foreshadowed by Britain's unsuccessful EEC application in 1961. Forewarned of Britain's intentions, Australia and New Zealand started to coordinate economic policy. In 1966, they signed the New Zealand–Australia Free Trade Agreement and by the late 1970s the vast majority of trans-Tasman trade was already free of tariffs. Nevertheless, this period of economic transition, occasioned by Britain's move into Europe, was always going to be more difficult for New Zealand than Australia. By way of comparison, Wellington was more dependent on the British market, more reliant on staple agricultural exports and more closely identified with Britain than Canberra. While New Zealand pulled off a diplomatic coup by negotiating a special access agreement with the EEC for its farm produce until 1980,[25] it was clear that it had to diversify its export markets as a matter of urgency. In these new and challenging circumstances, New Zealand began to forge an independent foreign policy.

New global context

By the early 1980s, New Zealand foreign policy had matured and expanded. Wellington still had close links with Britain, but the nature of this linkage had significantly changed. New Zealand had intellectually moved from a world view that was rooted in London to one that was increasingly centred in Wellington. This development coincided with the complex, multifaceted and contested globalisation process. New Zealand was significantly reshaped in at least four areas of its foreign policy.

National identity
New Zealand has been redefining itself and how it relates to the external world. Extraordinary changes in New Zealand in the last two or three decades challenge the old view that it is a 'small corner of England out in the Pacific'.[26] Above all, there has been a recognition of the special constitutional and cultural position of Maori people (expressed in the Treaty of Waitangi in terms of *rangatiratanga* [dominion] and *kawanatanga* [government]),

which, although still incomplete, has reflected and facilitated a weaving of things Maori into all parts of New Zealand's society and institutions.

New Zealand now has two official languages: English and Maori. Today many New Zealanders have become accustomed to the idea that their children will learn Maori in schools, though its use was strongly discouraged in the past. Maori concepts have also been extended into law, policy and social institutions. And there has been a general acceptance of the idea of compensation for lands unjustly taken or purchased and for the recognition of rights conferred under the Treaty of Waitangi to the Maori people.[27] In 1995, there was even a formal apology from Queen Elizabeth II for the previous actions of the Crown. Then, in March 2004, New Zealand's first dedicated Maori television station was launched.[28]

It should be emphasised that globalisation is a key driver in the revival of the indigenous rights and culture of New Zealand. While access to symbols of globalisation, such as the internet, remains uneven, particularly in rural New Zealand, this technology has, in the words of one observer, provided 'unprecedented opportunities' for Maori to project its language and culture, nationally and internationally.[29] The fact that New Zealand has one of the highest rates of computer ownership in the world has also lent momentum to this change.

A new sense of national identity has been further affected by the many new links New Zealand is building to other parts of the Pacific and the Asia-Pacific region. These ties have been forged for economic and diplomatic purposes. Languages for this region are now being taught in New Zealand schools. Many students from Asia-Pacific locales are studying in New Zealand universities.

In light of these changes New Zealand governments, whether involving National or Labour, evidently believe they have a mandate to strengthen the country's international commitment to promote human rights. As one of the founding members of the UN, New Zealand strongly advocated the inclusion of human rights in the UN Charter. It was also closely involved in the drafting of the Universal Declaration of Human Rights in 1948.

With the proliferation of civil conflicts in the post-Cold War era, the promotion of human rights has gained a new strategic significance. As Mary Robinson, the former UN high commissioner for human rights, has noted: 'Today's human rights abuses are the cause of tomorrow's conflicts.'[30]

Since New Zealand is engaged in a ground-breaking attempt to improve relations between Maori and Pakeha through the treaty settlement process, it has become conscious that it has a distinctive contribution to make internationally in the field of indigenous rights and ethnic conflict. Certainly, New Zealand has been actively involved in the drafting of the UN's Rights of Indigenous Peoples treaty. But international efforts in this area could be complicated by domestic political divisions over the Clark government's attempt to reconcile Pakeha and Maori aspirations in the Foreshore and Seabed legislation of 2004.[31]

Economic liberalisation
Despite its small size, New Zealand is a country with global economic interests. In the 1980s, New Zealand began to liberalise and reform its economy.

As part of this process, it signed a series of agreements with Australia in 1983 known as Closer Economic Relations (CER). This is arguably the most comprehensive trade agreement in existence and spans a range of areas. These include free trade in most goods, market harmonisation in services and capital, mutual recognition of many standards and the creation of an open labour market.[32]

CER has substantially benefited both countries. Trade between Australia and New Zealand, for example, has increased by over 400 per cent since 1983.[33] Australia is now New Zealand's biggest export market, taking at least 21 per cent of its exports, and New Zealand is currently the third largest market for Australian exports. Australia has also become New Zealand's primary source of investment capital, with Australian companies owning many of the key institutions in major sections of the New Zealand economy, such as banking and the mass media.

But globalisation has dramatically expanded the range of international opportunities for the New Zealand economy far beyond the CER market of around 24 million people. Today, New Zealand trades with more than 150 countries and is widely regarded as having one of the most open economies amongst the Organisation for Economic Cooperation and Development (OECD) countries. Moreover, New Zealand was one of the chief beneficiaries of the 1994 Uruguay General Agreement on Tariffs and Trade (GATT) round which began to liberalise trade in agriculture. It also has a lot to gain from the further liberalisation of trade in agriculture that was agreed at Geneva as part of the Doha Round of world trade talks in early August 2004. That could be worth something 'in the order of $1 billion a year'[34] to the New Zealand dairy industry alone.

While the WTO is reviled by many opponents of globalisation for weakening the nation-state, it has actually had the opposite effect in some areas. Consider, for instance, the new rules that the WTO introduced for settling trade disputes between states. Far from weakening New Zealand's national sovereignty, these rules have in a sense actually enhanced it by leveling the playing field for small, less powerful trading nations. The WTO disputes resolution mechanism is binding and sets parameters for a country to pursue a trade dispute against another over a trade problem. That allows the dispute to be sealed off from the rest of the bilateral relationship. Since the mid-1990s, New Zealand has used the machinery of the WTO to resolve disputes with some large trade partners: the EU, Canada and, with Australia, the US over lamb. To date, New Zealand has had a 100 per cent success rate without apparently damaging the relations with any of the parties involved.

Moreover, both of the major political parties in New Zealand have identified trade liberalisation as a key foreign policy objective. The decision of the Labour–Alliance government to raise income tax in 1999 and its refusal to match Australia's reduction of the corporate tax rate to 30 per cent was criticised by some of the political opposition parties as undermining New Zealand's competitiveness as a location for foreign investment. On the other hand, since taking office in 1999, Labour has signed free-trade agreements with Hong Kong and Singapore, and commenced trilateral Closer Economic Partnership (CEP) negotiations with Chile and Singapore in early 2003. It is also negotiating free-trade agreements with China and Thailand, and is looking forward to the launching of negotiations in November 2004 for an Association of South East Asian Nations (ASEAN)-CER free-trade pact.[35] In addition, the Clark government remains keen to conclude a free-trade agreement with the US after Australia moved outside the CER framework to pursue this type of arrangement with Washington. The Australian move seems to reflect exasperation inside the Howard government with both the economic and defence directions of the New Zealand government.

In addition, people-to-people contacts between New Zealand and the rest of the world are rapidly expanding. The declining cost of international travel and startling advances in communications technology has made geography less of an obstacle than previously. In 2002, the number of tourists visiting New Zealand during a twelve-month period exceeded the two million mark for the first time. This came only a decade after New Zealand had first recorded a million visitors in a year.[36]

The pursuit of security
Even before the end of the Cold War, New Zealand demonstrated it was prepared to adopt a distinctive approach to security matters. Strains within the Western alliance began to appear in the mid-1980s when the non-nuclear Labour government led by David Lange refused to allow unrestricted access to New Zealand ports by US naval vessels with nuclear propulsion or arms. The US responded by excluding New Zealand from ANZUS and suspending the exchange of strategic information and allied exercises with Wellington. Thereafter, the US described New Zealand as a friend, but not an ally.[37]

For the first decade or so of the post-Cold War era, the ANZUS rupture did not seem to affect the capacity of New Zealand to work cooperatively with Australia and the US in the security realm. Wellington backed the US-led coalition against Saddam Hussein in the Persian Gulf War of 1990–91; the US–UN humanitarian intervention in Somalia, 1992–93; and worked closely together with Australia to achieve a peace settlement in Bougainville in 1998. Furthermore, New Zealand's forces served under Australian command in East Timor as part of the International Force in East Timor (INTERFET) and close cooperation between both military forces has continued under the UN Transitional Administration in East Timor (UNTAET).

According to the deputy secretary of the Australian Defence Department, New Zealand's very rapid and professional commitment to support INTERFET made 'a massive impression' in Canberra.[38] New Zealand has also been a strong supporter of the Australian-led multinational force, the Regional Assistance Mission to the Solomon Islands (RAMSI), which intervened in July 2003 to restore law and order at the behest of the Solomon Islands government in the South Pacific.[39]

Nevertheless, the absence of the discipline of working together within the ANZUS framework has helped to generate different strategic outlooks between non-nuclear New Zealand, on the one hand, and Australia and the US on the other. These differences of strategic perspective began to surface with the election of the Labour–Alliance coalition in 1999.

From the beginning of her period in office, Clark made it clear that she did not regard New Zealand and Australia as a 'single strategic entity'.[40] In May 2000, the new Labour government abandoned the option negotiated by the previous National government to purchase twenty-eight F-16 fighter planes from the US on the grounds that the F-16s were too expensive for a country of New Zealand's size and military capability.

Twelve months later the government completed its review of New Zealand's defence strategy. Citing 'an incredibly benign strategic environment', three major defence decisions were made: New Zealand's air combat and strike capability would be abandoned; the navy would be restricted to two frigates and some basic transport and coastal patrol vessels; and the army would receive the bulk of government expenditure, some NZ$700 million to provide it with high-tech communications equipment and about one hundred new Armoured Personnel Carriers (APCs).[41]

The government argued that these changes were intended to provide New Zealand with a modern defence force that could contribute more effectively to international peacekeeping operations. Few would dispute New Zealand's role in UN peacekeeping. In 2003, for example, it had over 800 military personnel serving in thirteen UN-authorised peace support or humanitarian missions, including the Middle East, Sierra Leone and Mozambique.

But while New Zealand peacekeepers certainly needed the new equipment earmarked for the army, it was questionable whether these extra resources should be seen as the trade-off for the downgrading of the country's air force and naval capabilities. The new civil conflicts of the post-Cold War era generally require a mix of military capabilities, including air power, from contributors to international peacekeeping operations. If the Clark government deployed its new vehicles in a peacekeeping situation, it would have to depend entirely on other nations to provide the air cover that such deployments require.[42]

The new New Zealand approach to defence has angered and alarmed Australia, and to a lesser extent, the US. By presiding over what is seen as a serious degradation of New Zealand's military capabilities, it was argued that the Clark government may have jeopardised Wellington's future ability to contribute to ANZAC Alliance military operations.[43] With the recent decline in New Zealand military power projection capabilities, many Australians could believe that New Zealand, the twenty-first richest country in the world, was simply not prepared to assume a fair burden for their common defence.

New Zealand's decision to cancel its scheduled purchase of US F-16 combat aircraft was cited as a case in point. Some Australian media commentators have described the government's defence policy as the 'bludger's option'. While the Howard government has been more publicly restrained in its comments, it did make it clear there would be 'domestic and international consequences' flowing from New Zealand's new defence policy.⁴⁴ In 2004, the Howard government expressed its displeasure by signing a bilateral free-trade agreement that excluded New Zealand.

New Zealand and the post-9/11 security setting
After the dark side of globalisation struck, with devastating attacks on the World Trade Center and the Pentagon on 11 September 2001, President George W. Bush declared war on what was called global terrorism. Two New Zealanders were among the 3000 people killed on that fateful day. President Bush characterised the new conflict as a struggle between 'good and evil' and said 'either you are with us or you are with the terrorists'.⁴⁵

The response of the New Zealand government was substantial, but measured. New Zealand, according to the prime minister, pledged itself to making a 'a solid contribution' to the international effort against terrorism.⁴⁶

This contribution included: the deployment of a New Zealand Special Air Services (SAS) unit and an air force Hercules aeroplane to Afghanistan; the use of an ANZAC frigate, *Te Kaha*, an Orion surveillance aircraft and 242 navy and air force personnel in a Canadian-led force patrolling the Arabian Sea and the Gulf of Oman; the allocation of NZ$30 million over three years to boost New Zealand's domestic counter-terrorism measures in police, customs, immigration, intelligence and defence areas;⁴⁷ and the passing of the Terrorism Suppression Bill to conform with UN Security Council resolutions to tighten legislative measures against funding, harbouring, or otherwise assisting terrorist groups.

This antiterrorist legislation had the support of all parties in parliament, except the Greens. Mr Keith Locke, the foreign affairs spokesperson for the Green Party, warned that the bill's provisions undermined individual liberty and threatened lawful protests. But while a democracy must be careful not to subvert itself in a struggle with terrorism, New Zealand seems less vulnerable than others in this regard. It is a small society in which anonymity is difficult.

But the Clark government's support for the war on terror did not extend to backing a US-led invasion of Iraq in 2003. Wellington stated it could not support military action to disarm Iraq's alleged weapons of mass destruction that lacked any explicit UN Security Council authorisation. Here, the Clark government parted company with two traditional allies,

Australia and Britain, and drew some domestic criticism for indulging in a frivolous moral exercise that needlessly jeopardised New Zealand's national interests. According to the government's critics, the terrorist bomb blasts in Bali in October 2002, killing three New Zealanders and 190 Australians, and the reluctance of the Bush administration to negotiate a free-trade deal with New Zealand, confirmed that the government was not doing enough in the war against terrorism. But Prime Minister Helen Clark told an Australian audience that 'per capita, we've probably made one of the highest contributions to the military effort against terrorism',[48] and that New Zealand's capacity to take an independent stance on key international issues, such as the US invasion of Iraq, should not be exchanged for hypothetical economic or political benefits.

Multilateral diplomacy

Since 1945, New Zealand has signed up to all the major UN treaties and ratified virtually every key UN convention. It is also one of a small band of countries that has consistently paid its UN membership dues on time. These are achievements that some of the more powerful members of the UN cannot claim.

In the era of globalisation, New Zealand has continued to uphold the notion of a rules-based international order and to firmly support the UN as the embodiment of the multilateral process. Successive New Zealand governments, particularly during the post-Cold War period, seem to believe that globalisation is reinforcing multilateralism, and creating a more level playing field for small states like New Zealand to participate in global forums and forge new constituencies in support of core national goals. This is a 'can do' approach to global diplomacy.[49] It rejects the realist view that international influence is largely dependent on the possession of power.

Certainly, New Zealand has shown a presence on the international stage that is out of all proportion to its size. Despite lacking economic, military and political leverage, the country has secured a number of high-profile diplomatic positions during the post-Cold War period. It cannot be ruled out that New Zealand's refusal to abandon its non-nuclear stance in the face of US pressure in the second half of the 1980s contributed to this. In 1993, New Zealand acceded to one of the non-permanent seats on the UN Security Council; Don McKinnon, former New Zealand foreign minister, was subsequently appointed to the position of Secretary General of the Commonwealth; former New Zealand prime minister, Mike Moore, won a three-year 'split term' as director general of the WTO.[50]

The New Zealand approach to multilateralism in the era of globalisation can be distinguished from that of old allies like Britain and Australia. These countries have tended to behave as if the post-Cold War international system was unipolar, and that globalisation was centred on the US, the world's only superpower. According to this view, accessing the benefits of globalisation largely depends on achieving close relations with Washington.

Unlike New Zealand, Britain and Australia see themselves, to differing degrees, as middle-range powers. By presenting themselves as staunch allies of the US, the governments of Tony Blair and John Howard anticipate political, military, and commercial favours coming their way as well as increased influence in global institutions such as the UN and the WTO, and greater respect and recognition from regional great powers like China.[51]

These differences in global perspective have had consequences for both the style and substance of New Zealand's diplomacy. In terms of presentation, New Zealand has been more forthright in supporting multilateral initiatives than some of its allies. For example, Wellington's strong public support for developments like the 1997 Ottawa Treaty banning antipersonnel landmines, the recent establishment of the International Criminal Court (ICC), and the 2004 ruling by the International Court of Justice (ICJ) concerning the illegal status of Israel's new security barrier, largely coincided with the positions of Britain and Australia, but these countries prefer a 'quiet diplomacy' style on those issues where they disagree with Washington.

With regard to the substance of foreign policy, New Zealand has found itself at odds with the Bush administration and its allies on at least three major international issues. The first concerns the Kyoto Protocol on climate change, which seeks to place international limits on global warming. Shortly after taking office, President George W. Bush announced that the US was withdrawing from the Kyoto agreement, citing fears for the effect it would have on the US economy. Australia almost immediately followed America's lead. The Australian environment minister, Senator Robert Hill, was 'dead' without the US's agreement. But New Zealand disagreed and made it clear that it intended to stick by the Kyoto Protocol.[52]

The second issue concerns President Bush's decision to proceed with a National Missile Defense (NMD) system. This system is intended to protect the US and its allies from ballistic missile attacks from 'rogue' states such as North Korea and Iran. The New Zealand foreign minister, Phil Goff, roundly condemned the concept. Citing concerns of China and Russia, Goff said a missile screen would not necessarily protect the US or anyone else from terrorist acts like those on 9/11 and 'risks undermining the current network of nuclear arms control and disarmament treaties'.[53] In contrast, the Blair and Howard governments have expressed support for the NMD scheme, and also a willingness to participate in its implementation.

The third issue relates to US policy towards Iraq. As previously noted, the Clark government refused to support the pre-emptive use of military force in Iraq by the US and its allies unless it was sanctioned by the UN Security Council. The New Zealand prime minister argued that an unauthorised attack would undermine international law and play into the hands of terrorist groups like al-Qaeda. The precarious security situation in Iraq since the formal end of hostilities in May 2003 presumably reinforces the New Zealand government's conviction that unilateralism simply cannot be an effective tool in dealing with problems like terrorism in a globalising world.

Conclusion

In the last two decades, New Zealand foreign policy has faced a period of substantial readjustment. The advent of intensified globalisation coincided with profound changes in New Zealand's national identity and its role in the world. Sweeping deregulation of the economy and an ambitious attempt to improve relations between Maori and Pakeha through the Crown's recognition of indigenous rights has been linked to reinvigorated New Zealand support for international human rights, the expansion of free-trade and multilateral institutions. At the same time, New Zealand has moved towards closer relations with the Asia-Pacific rim and adopted a non-nuclear security policy.

On the basis of the evidence presented here, there is little or no support for the hyperglobalist claim that the forces of globalisation have emasculated the sovereign state in New Zealand. In the preglobalisation era, it was clear there was never a time when the New Zealand state exercised absolute and exclusive sovereignty. For much of its existence, New Zealand sovereignty has been constrained by its geographical isolation, a close political identification with Britain or simply the realities of a hierarchical international arena. Therefore, New Zealand policy makers have tended to treat the advent of globalisation as a new constraint to be navigated, rather than a fundamental threat to the state per se.

At the same time, the New Zealand experience provides little support for the sceptics' view that the sovereign state remained largely unaffected by globalisation. In a globalising world, New Zealand has witnessed, like many other states, the blurring of the distinction between 'foreign' and 'domestic' issues that is so central to the Westphalian state. The main engine of this process is technology. It is technical changes and efficiencies of scale and communication that have made state-centred solutions to problems, such as trade, global warming, the spread of infectious diseases or the rise of transnational crime, relatively inefficient, and prompted the proliferation of links across borders as well as the emergence of significant non-state actors. For a small state, like New Zealand, the benefits of multilateral cooperation far outweigh the costs of trying to go it alone in an interconnected world.

Rather, the New Zealand example seems to most closely correspond to the transformationalist school of thought whereby the country's foreign policy has been reshaped by the transformation of the New Zealand state in conditions of globalisation.

This perspective maintains that the role of the sovereign state is being redefined by globalisation because countries themselves increasingly recognise they are confronted by new global forces beyond their ability to control. In the circumstances, states risk being marginalised unless they are prepared to engage in hard-headed multilateralism in order to exert some sovereign influence over these new forces.

Viewed in this way, New Zealand's diplomacy has been remarkably effective. It seems to confirm that influence in an interconnected world does not entirely depend on 'hard power'.[54] New Zealand has demonstrated an active presence in the global arena that is out of all proportion to its size. In a number of key international institutions such as the UN, the Commonwealth, and the WTO, leadership positions have been occupied by New Zealanders. It seems that by de-emphasising the significance of geography and size, and redefining the relationship between 'hard' and 'soft' power in world politics, globalisation has provided a small, developed state, like New Zealand, with new opportunities to promote its core values and interests in international institutions and forums that characterise the process. Thus, while New Zealand sovereignty has been subject to the forces of globalisation, it has also served as an agent of globalisation, for both self-interested and normative reasons.

The 'new war' against terrorism unleashed after 9/11 does little to disturb the general thrust of the Clark government's approach to globalisation, but it does highlight that the scope for compartmentalising New Zealand's security policy from other aspects of its interaction with key trading partners such as Australia may be diminishing. The point was underlined by the 2004 Australian-US free-trade agreement that excluded New Zealand. If the Clark government has paid an economic price for failing to fully recognise the link between defence and trade, it probably did so on the basis that New Zealand's ability to take a robust multilateralist position on key international issues such as the Iraq invasion should not be traded for hypothetical economic or political benefits. However, if Wellington listens more carefully to Canberra's concerns on New Zealand's defence policy, it could improve New Zealand-Australian security relations without compromising New Zealand's commitment to multilateralism.

Notes

1. Dr Boutros Boutros-Ghali, former UN secretary general, cited by Don McKinnon, 'New Zealand Sovereignty in an Interdependent World' in G.A. Wood and L.S. Leland, Jr (eds), *State and Sovereignty: Is the State in Retreat?* (Dunedin, University of Otago Press, 1997), p.7.
2. John Jackson, 'Sovereignty: A New Approach to an Outdated Concept', *American Journal of International Law*, 97, 4 (2003), p.3.
3. Max Weber cited in J. Hoffmann, *Beyond the State: An Introductory Critique* (Cambridge, Cambridge University Press, 1995), p.3.
4. Jan Scholte, 'The Globalization of World Politics' in John Baylis and Steve Smith (eds), *The Globalization of World Politics: An Introduction to International Relations* (Oxford, Oxford University Press, 2001), 2nd edition, p.14.
5. Ian Clark, *Globalization and Fragmentation* (Oxford, Oxford University Press, 1997), p.15.
6. Martin Shaw, *Theory of the Global State: Globality as Unfinished Revolution* (New York, Cambridge University Press, 2000), pp.11–12.
7. R. Schaeffer, *Understanding Globalization* (New York, Rowman and Littlefield, 2003), p.26.
8. Don McKinnon, 'New Zealand Sovereignty in an Interdependent World' in G. A. Wood and L.S. Leland, Jr (eds), *State and Sovereignty: Is the State in Retreat?*, p.11.
9. David Held and Anthony McGrew, *Global Transformations* (Cambridge, Polity Press, 1999), p.4.
10. David Held and Anthony McGrew, *Global Transformations*, p.6.
11. David Held and Anthony McGrew, *Global Transformations*, p.8.
12. P. Hirst and G. Thompson, *Globalization in Question* (Cambridge, Cambridge University Press, 1996), p.96; Nigel Haworth, 'Multinational Corporations and State Sovereignty' in G.A. Wood and L.S. Leland, Jr (eds), *State and Sovereignty: Is the State in Retreat?*, pp.80–82.
13. Nigel Haworth, 'Multinational Corporations and State Sovereignty', pp.80–81.

14 P. Hirst and G. Thompson, *Globalization in Question*, pp.96–8.
15 David Held and Anthony McGrew, *Global Transformations*, p.11.
16 Samuel Barkin, 'Resilience of the State', *Harvard International Review*, 22, 4 (2001), p.5.
17 John Henderson, 'New Zealand and the Foreign Policy of Small States' in Richard Kennaway and John Henderson (eds), *Beyond New Zealand. 11, Foreign Policy into the 1990s* (Auckland, Longman Paul, 1991), p.6.
18 Simon Upton, 'How New Zealand Sees Itself in the World', *New Zealand International Review*, 25, 4, July 2000, pp.9–10.
19 Steve Hoadley, 'Foreign Policy' in Raymond Miller (ed), *New Zealand Politics in Transition* (Auckland, Oxford University Press, 1997), p.299.
21 Bob Catley, *Waltzing with Maltilda: Should New Zealand Join Australia?* (Wellington, Dark Horse Publishing, 2001), pp.51–2.
22 Bob Catley, *Waltzing with Maltilda*, p.52.
23 Robert G. Patman (ed), *New Zealand and Britain: A Special Relationship in Transition* (Palmerston North, Dunmore Press, 1997), p.13.
24 Bob Catley, *Waltzing with Maltilda: Should New Zealand Join Australia?*, p.53.
25 Bruce Brown, 'From Bulk Purchase to Butter Disputes' in Robert G. Patman (ed), *New Zealand and Britain: A Special Relationship in Transition*, pp.41–66.
26 Ngaire Woods, 'Converging Challenges and Diverging Identities' in Robert G. Patman (ed), *New Zealand and Britain: A Special Relationship in Transition*, p.27.
27 Ngaire Woods, 'Converging Challenges and Diverging Identities', p.38.
28 *New Zealand Herald*, 29 March 2004.
29 Lawrence Zwimpfer, 'Digital Divide or Digital Opportunities—Two Sides of the Same Coin?', paper presented at UNESCO one-day seminar on *New Zealand and the World*, Royal Society of New Zealand, Wellington, 22 June 2001.
30 Mary Robinson cited in Ian Hill, 'New Zealand's International Human Rights Policy: A Small State Trying to Make a Difference', paper presented at a University of Otago seminar, 17 May 2002.
31 *New Zealand Herald*, 13 August 2004.
32 Bob Catley, *Waltzing with Maltilda*, pp.86–9.
33 *Australian Financial Review*, 14 April 2000.
34 Jim Sutton, New Zealand Trade Minister, cited in *New Zealand Herald*, 2 August 2004.
35 *New Zealand Herald*, 13 August 2004.
36 *Sunday Star Times*, Wellington, 22 December 2002.
37 Bob Catley, *Waltzing with Maltilda*, pp.53–4.
38 H. White, 'An Australian Viewpoint on Strategic Issues', paper presented at the 36th University of Otago Foreign Policy School, Dunedin, 29 June 2000.
39 *New Zealand Herald*, 18 February 2004.
40 Bob Catley, *Waltzing with Maltilda*, p.56.
41 *Otago Daily Times*, 12 April 2001.
42 *Dominion Post*, 12 September 2003.
43 David Dickens, 'The ANZAC Connection: Does the Australian-New Zealand Strategic

Relationship have a Future', paper presented at the 36th University of Otago Foreign Policy School, Dunedin, 29 June 2000.
44 Australian prime minister, John Howard, cited in Jenny Shipley, Leader of the Opposition, *National Party Press Release*, 31 July 2001.
45 President George W. Bush, speech to both houses of Congress, cited in CNN.com on 20 September 2001: www.cnn.com/2001/us09/20gen.america.under.attack/index.html.
46 Helen Clark, *Media Statement of the New Zealand Prime Minister*, 11 November 2002.
47 Phil Goff, 'Asia-Pacific Security Challenges', speech delivered to the 37th University of Otago Foreign Policy School, Dunedin, 28 June 2002.
48 *New Zealand Herald*, 9 July 2004.
49 Neil Walter, 'New Zealand's Changing Place in the World', *Record: New Zealand Foreign Affairs and Trade*, 9, 2 (2000).
50 *Japan Times*, 30 April 2000.
51 *Australian Financial Review*, 31 May 2000.
52 *Teletext National and World News*, 7 July 2001.
53 Phil Goff, 'New Challenges, New Approaches', speech delivered at the Annual Dinner of the New Zealand Institute of International Affairs, Wellington, 14 May 2001.
54 Joseph S. Nye Jr, *The Paradox of American Power: Why the World's Only Superpower Can't Go it Alone* (New York, Oxford University Press, 2002), pp.ix–xvi.

5

DIPLOMATIC 'INTERESTS'

Malcolm McKinnon

This chapter does not fall neatly under the rubric 'globalisation'. On the other hand it is about what might be called the first truly global profession—that of diplomacy.

In work I have done on New Zealand's foreign relations I have paid relatively little attention to the policy makers. My attention has been much more on policy itself. This was something that Rod Alley queried more than once, and the thought stayed with me. The query has taken a while to fertilise, perhaps because not a lot of such work has been done by others either. The most useful starting points are the introductions to the three volumes of *New Zealand in World Affairs*, published by the New Zealand Institute of International Affairs (NZIIA) in 1977, 1991 and 1999, by Alister McIntosh, Malcolm Templeton and Merv Norrish respectively—all practitioners of diplomacy it should be noted. Equally useful are Ian McGibbon's introductions to his two edited collections of informal officials' (if that is not an oxymoron) correspondence—*Undiplomatic Dialogue* and *Unofficial Channels*—as well as the contributions to the Ministry of Foreign Affairs' fiftieth anniversary commemoration volume, *An Eye, an Ear and a Voice*. That volume reproduces an address by McIntosh himself, the first secretary (1943 to 1966) of the then Department of External Affairs on the occasion of being awarded an honorary doctorate from the University of Canterbury.[1] Finally, the first volume of *Beyond New Zealand* had a contribution from George Laking, another practitioner; and one from John Henderson, a scholar turned practitioner.[2]

All these contributions are in the form of essays and this suggests, but perhaps no more, that there is scope for further enquiry. I say 'suggests' because if something hasn't been investigated very thoroughly it may mean that it will not repay thorough investigation. However, devoting a short chapter to the subject hardly constitutes 'thorough'. On the other hand, if it means that I manage to interest others in the worth of pursuing these questions I think it will be a chapter well justified.

One trigger to my own recent interest in the subject was reviewing the entries on diplomats and other participants in the conduct of New Zealand's foreign relations in volume five of the *Dictionary of New Zealand Biography* (*DNZB V*).³ Another trigger was work on the professionalisation of the Treasury, indeed I structured the Treasury history around the successive 'rise' of first the accountant, and then the economist.

Such analyses, if they are to be more than observation and description, need to be grounded in theory—even an historian can concede that, particularly, perhaps, when addressing political scientists. Marx provides one obvious starting point—the notion of officials as agents of a ruling class, or of dominant interests, a line of theorising which can be traced to the present day in writings invoking the ideas of political economy as a 'school'. Max Weber, with his interest in the rise of bureaucracies, provides an alternative emphasis, to which the public choice theorising first associated with writers such as Gordon Tullock and Patrick Buchanan, provides a counterpoint. The 'pure' version of this theory was not as illuminating for me as the glosses placed on it by scholars such as Hugh Heclo and Aaron Wildarvsky, in their justly renowned *The Private Government of Public Money*, and by Patrick Dunleavy, whose theorising about what fiscal bureaucrats do and why is particularly illuminating for any student of a government department of finance.⁴ Indeed there is a certain irony in using a theory applied by Treasury officials to explain the conduct of others, to explain the actions of Treasury officials themselves.

I think that such approaches can be useful for understanding diplomats and foreign ministries. While I am not going to dwell any more on the theory at this juncture, it will be in the background. In particular there is the 'rough and ready' idea that it can be useful, as a starting point, to assume that officials' actions can be illuminated by knowledge of their origins and socialisation, and that they act self-interestedly, albeit that that self-interest might include a degree of altruism.

Three 'clusters' of observations about the diplomatic profession in New Zealand might usefully be investigated in this fashion.

Collective biography

In the review of *DNZB V* article I looked at the 'first generation' of officials/diplomats (the term loosely applied), men (very few women) like Alister McIntosh, Bill Gilbert, Leslie Munro, 'Dick' Powles, Foss Shanahan, Steve Weir and J. V. Wilson. They hailed mostly from the lower middle class. Amongst the list of fathers' occupations for them and others of their generation were: accounts clerk, pharmacist, grocer, commercial traveller, storekeeper, telegraphist and police constable. As I argued in that review, 'Our representative diplomat . . . went to the local public primary and high school, then joined the workforce. Degree study at a state-funded university college was completed part-time, he did not participate in the "back and forth, New Zealand and England" routine of well-off New Zealanders—or for that matter, of Rhodes Scholars. He left New Zealand for the first-time when well into his twenties. From his thirties and older, in the late 1940s and 1950s, he became extensively involved in diplomacy and international relations.'[5]

These individuals were not recruited from the country's social or business elite. Did this foster deference to the powerful both in their own countries and elsewhere, or a robust independence of spirit? There is more evidence for the latter and George Laking, a contemporary of many of the inhabitants of *DNZB V*—as might be expected of someone who has passed 91 years of age!—has commented that New Zealand diplomats responded positively to the democratic and egalitarian temper of Washington DC. At the same time dealing with British and European diplomats and ministers whose social background and education would often have been privileged does not appear to have discomfited them.

The 'movers and shakers' of that generation, who had the most markedly working-class origins—W. B. Sutch (whose father was a carpenter) and Jack Lewin (whose father was an engine-driver and a unionist)—tended to be the most left-wing. Those whose political orientation was 'pink' rather than 'red' were mostly from the lower middle classes or the middle class proper.

We could also permit ourselves a 'nationality' analysis. These individuals were all New Zealand-born, often of New Zealand-born parents of British descent, and mostly Protestant—Shanahan was a noticeable exception in this latter respect. The combination provides almost too good a fit, the tone of New Zealand diplomacy in their generation being independent but not anti-British. The enthusiasm for the Commonwealth—the decolonised version of the Empire—sat comfortably with them as perhaps it still does with their descendants. So did support for other international organisations that were, to New Zealand eyes, variations on the Commonwealth theme—the South Pacific Commission, the Colombo Plan, and the United Nations.

Professionalism

Professions are about 'principles' but they are also about self-interest—more status, more influence, more money. To what extent can the story of the Department of External Affairs/Ministry of Foreign Affairs be seen as the story of a group of individuals who sought professional standing, and somewhat more than that of a 'public servant'? Comparisons can be made, not just with Treasury accountants and economists, but with doctors, engineers and scientists. I would point to two phases in the history of our diplomatic 'class' which are suggestive. McIntosh himself was clearly preoccupied with what he referred to as the 'craft' of diplomacy, and the relationship between that craft and the work of the universities in producing graduates. In his introduction to *Unofficial Channels*, which reproduces correspondence between Alister McIntosh and Frank Corner, George Laking and Foss Shanahan, Ian McGibbon comments, 'all four correspondents had common objectives in mind . . . that New Zealand have a department at home and a diplomatic network abroad that could secure and enhance its international interests; that its representatives should have the skill and commitment to help shape national policies . . .'[6]

What is the balance between the 'public' and 'private' good that the pursuit of such goals served? It was axiomatic to the officials that more highly trained and more influential officials would be good for the country. Would better paid ones also be good for it? At the time that McIntosh addressed the University of Canterbury, salary relativities were a live issue. Officials in the Foreign and Commonwealth Affairs (FCA) in the Department of External Affairs sought a solution to this problem by establishing a professional association. It was felt that the existing occupational classes were meaningless, and that the nature of the work carried out by FCA officers, and in particular the work they carried out overseas, was sufficiently distinctive to merit recognition as a separate occupational class that received commensurate remuneration—which, unsurprisingly for a public choice theorist, translated into increases.[7] The Association that was eventually to be formed at the end of 1970 was a more modest affair, but it seems fair to reckon that this was a classic instance of a group of individuals seeking to 'professionalise' in a fashion which would enhance both their status and their rewards.

Ministers and (diplomatic) officials and diplomatic history

My third topic also draws on public choice approaches. It was also touched on by McIntosh in 1965 when he stressed, to his university audience, that 'the diplomat must always remember that he is a servant, that he possesses power without substance. As the slave stood beside [the conqueror] so the civil servant stands in relation to his government.'[8] A public choice framework suggests that any change which gives officials more authority and autonomy will be regarded favourably, whilst changes which see the balance reversed will be regarded unfavourably—and that this might be the case irrespective of the significance for diplomatic relations as such. Three episodes throw light on this notion.

The first took place in 1945, which McIntosh himself, in 1965, identified as 'perhaps the golden period of New Zealand's external relations', with the drafting of the Charter of the United Nations, and the early years of that world organisation. McIntosh's 'golden period' was a 'magic moment' for a barely decade-old 'independent' New Zealand diplomacy. But it had very little significance for the structure of New Zealand's international situation in 1945 or shortly thereafter, with a weakened Great Britain, American hegemony in the Pacific, and a United Nations soon to be paralysed by the Cold War.

The second episode was the election of the third Labour government in late 1972, and the energising approach brought to the conduct of foreign relations by the incoming prime minister Norman Kirk, in conjunction with the new Secretary of Foreign Affairs, Frank Corner. Norman Kirk's initiatives in 1972—the ending of involvement in Vietnam, the recognition of mainland China, the reopening of an embassy in Moscow—gave diplomats scope to both advise and act in ways that had been at a discount during the Holyoake years. But the structural change—détente—was already under way. New Zealand had largely pulled out of Vietnam in 1971, 1972 was the year of Nixon's trip to China, while his 1973 trip to Moscow had been foreshadowed. On the economic front, Jack Marshall had secured a trade agreement with the European Economic Community 'six', including France, giving Kirk more scope than his predecessors to take a strong stance against French Pacific nuclear testing.

The third episode was the election of the Labour government in 1984 and the adoption of the antinuclear policy. In the sense that the new government was less congenial to the diplomats in Foreign Affairs than the outgoing one, 1984 was the reverse of 1972 (and interestingly the reverse for Foreign Affairs as compared with the Treasury). Official advice was ignored, but officials also suffered directly from the change in policy. It was the professional environment and standing of New Zealand diplomats and foreign ministry officials in Wellington, Washington, and elsewhere which was affected more than anything or anyone else by the 'cold war' imposed on New Zealand by the Reagan administration. Of such discomfort the average antinuclear New Zealand voter felt not a trace, and the leadership of the new government not much more—or not enough.

Readers may recognise that I am over-yolking the egg, but the underlying point is an important one. Self-interest may not be the only diplomatic interest, but it is one, amongst diplomats as amongst nations, and our understanding of New Zealand's diplomats, its diplomatic interests, and its diplomatic history, will be deepened if we keep this in mind.

Notes

1 A.D. McIntosh et al, *New Zealand in World Affairs* I (Wellington, Price Milburn, 1977); Malcolm McKinnon (ed), *New Zealand in World Affairs* II (Wellington, New Zealand Institute of International Affairs, 1991); Brown, Bruce (ed), *New Zealand in World Affairs* III (Wellington, Victoria University Press, 1999); Ian McGibbon (ed), *Undiplomatic Dialogue* (Auckland, Auckland University Press, 1993); Ian McGibbon (ed), *Unofficial Channels* (Wellington, Victoria University Press, 1999); Malcolm Templeton (ed), *An Eye, an Ear and a Voice* (Wellington, Ministry of Foreign Affairs and Trade, 1993), p.19.

2 John Henderson, Keith Jackson and Richard Kennaway, *Beyond New Zealand: The Foreign Policy of a Small State* (Auckland, Methuen, 1980); John Henderson and Richard Kennaway, *Beyond New Zealand. II, Foreign Policy into the 1980s* (Auckland, Longman Paul, 1991).

3 *New Zealand International Review*, 26, 3 (2001), pp.27–9.

4 Hugh Heclo and Aaron Wildarvsky, *The Private Government of Public Money* (London, Macmillan, 1974); Patrick Dunleavy, *Democracy, Bureaucracy and Public Choice* (New York, Prentice Hall, 1991).

5 *New Zealand International Review*, 26, 3 (2001), pp.27–9.

6 Ian McGibbon, *Unofficial Channels* (Auckland, Auckland University Press, 1999), p.9, pp.35–7.

7 See Foreign Service Association 1/1, especially memo of 17 November 1969.

8 Malcolm Templeton, *An Eye, an Ear and a Voice*, (Wellington, Ministry of Foreign Affairs and Trade, 1993) p.21.

NEW ZEALAND'S ROLE IN THE PACIFIC

6

SECURITY IN OCEANIA IN THE POST-9/11 AND -BALI ERA

John Henderson

The Bali bombing of 12 October 2002, which killed more than 200 people, eighty-eight of them Australians, was Oceania's 9/11. It brought about a profound change in regional and particularly Australian security thinking. This chapter focuses on the repercussions of the attack for Australian and New Zealand perceptions of their Pacific Island neighbourhood. While the blast took place in Indonesia the impact on the adjoining region of Oceania (defined as Australia, New Zealand, and the island states of the South Pacific) has been considerable.

First, this chapter will examine an indirect, but nevertheless the most visible, consequence of the bombing: the 2003 Australian-led intervention in the Solomon Islands (which became known as RAMSI—Regional Assistance Mission to the Solomon Islands). Secondly, it will consider New Zealand's diminished role in Pacific security affairs—in comparison with Australia's enhanced commitment. Thirdly, it will analyse the extent of the on-going terrorist threat to Oceania. The chapter concludes with a call for a greater regional response to security issues which could provide an alternative to Australia (and to a lesser extent New Zealand) taking on a continuing role as regional policeman.

For Australia 2003 marked a change in Pacific policy from 'hands-off' to direct intervention. The profound nature of the change is highlighted by the differing responses to the Solomon Islands' pleas for assistance in 2000 and 2003. In the first half of 2000 both Australia and New Zealand rejected repeated calls for security assistance from Bartholomew Ulufa'alu, the democratically elected Solomon Islands prime minister, on the grounds that there was no peace to keep. There was also concern about the lack of an effective 'exit' strategy. This marked the first time a Pacific Island neighbour had asked for Australian and New Zealand assistance and been refused. The result was the armed uprising of June 2000, which forced Ulufa'alu's resignation and effectively overthrew a democratically elected government. In stark contrast, three years later Australia responded to a similar request for help from the Solomon's government of Allan Kemakeza by leading a massive regional force of over 2000 police and military personnel.

What changed between 2000 and 2003? It was the Bali bombing which shook Australia out of viewing Oceania with benign neglect. This was replaced with a policy of active intervention in a region which was now considered a threat to Australian security. Concern was expressed about the threat posed by the so-called 'arc of instability' stretching across Australia's north from Indonesia and the Philippines through Papua New Guinea (PNG), Bougainville, the Solomon Islands, Vanuatu and New Caledonia to Fiji. The Australian government's willingness to respond with military force if necessary to regional trouble spots signalled a new Australian version of the United States's (US) Monroe Doctrine. Australia reserves the right to intervene if it considers its security interests are threatened.

To help placate regional concern about Australian muscle flexing the new strategy was given the non-threatening title of 'cooperative intervention'. This was intervention with a smile rather than a snarl, to be undertaken with the cooperation of the country itself, and with assistance from other regional states.

The efforts to avoid accusations of Australian neo-colonialism arising from the Solomon Islands intervention have set a precedent for future regional operations. The Solomons 'formula' consists of the following steps:

- a request from a Pacific Island government for security assistance (Of course the nature of the 'request' may be open to question. For the Solomon Islands it may have been a request it could not refuse to make. Indeed, the speed and the scale of the intervention suggest the request and response were, at least to some extent, 'pre cooked'.)
- legal cover for the intervention, which may include special legislation passed through the island parliament
- regional endorsement through the main regional organisation, the Pacific Island Forum, if necessary through a special meeting of Forum foreign ministers
- wide regional participation in the intervention force. The significant police component should enable most island states to contribute to the force. Australia, New Zealand and other states with armed

forces, particularly Fiji, may be looked to for as much military back-up as necessary.

The extent to which effective regional consultation can take place will depend on the time available, which in turn will reflect the nature of the crisis. In the case of the Solomon Island intervention the decision-making process stretched over several weeks (or even months if the Australian Strategic Policy Institute (ASPI) think tank report, which provided the justification, is taken into account). However, effective intervention following, for example, a further coup in Fiji is likely to require an immediate response. Such crises may produce a case of act first and legitimise later. Australian foreign minister Alexander Downer has hinted that pre-emptive action may be necessary. 'There is a point where we can't sit by . . . where we have to engage with these countries and get the problem fixed.'[1]

The extent to which the Solomons intervention becomes a precedent for other similar operations will depend on how successful it is considered to have been. In military and police terms it clearly succeeded, as the militia forces offered little or no resistance, and law and order was quickly restored.

However, resolving deep-rooted political issues will be a more lengthy process. This will not be helped by the propping up, at least in the short term, of the ineffective and corrupt government headed by Prime Minister Allan Kemakeza. Nor can the shortcomings be overcome for the long term by 'embedded' Australian officials. If Solomon Islanders are not running their own affairs they have, in effect, been recolonised.

A key problem for future stability in Melanesia is the artificial nature of the countries in terms of their geography and political system. For instance, the Solomon Islands is the product of the colonial era, when boundaries were drawn which largely ignored local custom. After nearly twenty-five years of independence there is little or no sense of Solomon Island nationalism. In the fragmented society which characterises Melanesia the centralised Westminster system has proved to be unsuitable. The future may lie in a decentralised federal structure.

The implications of this conclusion are important, but seem to have been largely overlooked. Putting the Solomon Islands back the way it was before the 2000 uprising is not a 'solution'. Indeed it can be argued that it is not the Solomon Islanders but the Westminster political system, inherited at the time of independence, which has produced a 'failed state'.

Where to next?

There have been Pacific concerns that the Solomon Islands are just the curtain-raiser for future similar Australian-led interventions. Australian prime minister John Howard has warned that the 'sovereignty' of a number of Pacific Island states is at risk because they are on the point of collapse due to corruption and lawlessness, and he has suggested that multilateral interventions might be necessary.[2] He has stressed the need for Australia to maintain the capability to undertake future interventions.[3] There are plans for several hundred Australian police to be deployed to PNG.

After a period of relative stability, Vanuatu politics is again becoming turbulent. The possibility that it could be the next to 'benefit' from intervention is heightened by the fact that, being smaller, it would be manageable in a way PNG would not.

Fiji faces an on-going constitutional crisis. The military remains deeply divided. But, as noted earlier, any plans for a further coup must now factor in the possibility of Australian and New Zealand military intervention to reverse the coup. It is noteworthy that Fiji has an Australian as chief of police.

Tonga also faces an uncertain future under an ageing and ailing monarch. It is a problem which, in contrast to the Melanesian states noted, Australia would prefer to leave to New Zealand to resolve. It may be a very difficult call to make. If, for instance, disorder broke out as a result of a violent clampdown on prodemocracy supporters, what action should the New Zealand government take? To do nothing would be ignoring the pleas of a friendly regional country in its hour of need (as happened to the Solomon Islands in 2000); but to respond and prop up the government would be to suppress democracy.

New Zealand's secondary role

Australia's more assertive approach to Pacific affairs has had the effect of relegating New Zealand to a secondary role. It marks the end of an era when it was widely believed that New Zealand had a better feel for the region than Australia. The lead role New Zealand played in the 1990s in resolving the conflict arising from Bougainville's attempt to break from PNG marked a high point in New Zealand regional leadership. It was privately resented by Australian officials, who (unofficially) objected to New Zealand's intrusion onto their 'patch'. Future lead roles for New Zealand in Oceania are likely to be restricted to Polynesia.

There is much more at stake here than petty trans-Tasman jealousy and one-upmanship. To be fully effective in the region New Zealand needs to be seen to be acting independently, and not as a surrogate for Australia. It was because New Zealand did not carry the baggage of the main backer of the PNG military (Australia) that it was seen to be more impartial, and was able to take the lead role in resolving the Bougainville conflict. It is not in Australia's or New Zealand's interests that New Zealand's ability to undertake similar actions be compromised.

Compared with Australia, New Zealand has a number of advantages in its relationship with the island states: small size (therefore less threatening); significant Pacific Island population (around 6 per cent, or over 20 per cent Polynesian when indigenous Maori are included); distance from Asia (it is therefore perceived as less of a threat and more a part of Oceania). New Zealand's more relaxed style (compared with Australia's business-like approach) is well regarded by Pacific governments. These advantages are lost if New Zealand's foreign policy is viewed as an extension of Australia's. Such views are reinforced when a New Zealand foreign minister accompanies his Australian counterpart on regional visits transported in an Australian air force plane. Inevitably New Zealand will be seen to be one step behind and following in Australia's footsteps. Images are important in politics and international relations. New Zealand should avoid being seen as the 'deputy' to the US 'deputy sheriff'.

Although the Australian and New Zealand prime ministers, John Howard and Helen Clark, enjoy a good personal relationship the governments have different views of their strategic environments. It is no longer accurate to refer to Australia and New Zealand forming a single strategic entity. Australia is preoccupied by its close proximity to Asia. New Zealand does not have to contend with boat people. Australia gives priority to its alliance with the US. New Zealand has learned to live without the Australia, New Zealand, US alliance (ANZUS). In 2003 Australia joined the US and Britain in the invasion of Iraq. New Zealand did not, although it contributed to the reconstruction.

Australia is not alone in increasingly 'looking North' to Asia. So too, increasingly, do Pacific Island (particularly Melanesian) states. For Australia and New Zealand it is a reminder that Pacific Island states have other options when seeking aid and other support. There were reports that, before the Australian-led intervention, the Solomon Island government was considering asking Indonesia to send armed forces to help restore law and order.[4] There are limits to which the requirements of 'good governance' (that is, the Western form of democracy and public administration) can be insisted upon as conditions for aid. China and Taiwan compete for regional influence. Japan, the region's economic superpower, is taking on a leadership role through the hosting of the three-yearly Pacific Island leader's summit.

Does terrorism constitute a threat to Oceania?

Is terrorism a real threat to the Pacific, or does it merely provide convenient cover to justify an enhanced Australian (and to a lesser extent New Zealand) military and police presence? Terrorist acts are not a likely prospect according to the the US or the island states themselves. In 2002 the chief of the US Pacific Command, Dennis Blair, gave the region a 'low priority' rating for attention in regard to terrorist threats.[5] The former Cook Islands prime minister, Geoffrey Henry, went further with the comment that the terrorism issue was of 'little relevance' to most Pacific Islanders.[6] Pacific concerns about economic and environmental security do not feature in the war on terrorism.

A common criticism of military and security planners is that they prepare to fight past conflicts rather than new types of future threats. Nevertheless the top three threats—tourist centres, aircraft hijacking, and ethnic strife—all remain highly relevant to Oceania. Other terrorist-related concerns include surrogate targets, transit points, governance and money laundering.

Tourist centres
The Bali bombing and the Mombasa attack highlight the risk of attacks on tourist centres. The terrorist target is not the country itself, but the foreign nationals who are there as tourists. This was Australians in the case of Bali, and Israelis in Mombasa. Tourism is a major industry in a number of Pacific Islands, such as Fiji, New Caledonia, Vanuatu, and Palau, but it is not on the scale of Bali. Most resorts have tightened security, but still present relatively 'soft' targets to terrorist groups. Tightening security around tourist centres has been an increasingly important part of the Pacific Island's security agenda.

Hijacking
The 9/11 attack on the US demonstrated with chilling effect how hijacked civilian aircraft can be transformed into guided missiles. Hijackings continue to present a credible threat to the Pacific. At the time of the May 1987 coup in Fiji an Air New Zealand aircraft was hijacked at Nadi airport. As all Pacific Island states—with the exception of Tokelau—have airports, they are potential targets for hijackers. But the risk is clearly higher in states with significant international airports such as Nadi. All Pacific states have tightened airport security in the wake of 9/11, but despite considerable assistance from aid donors, antiterrorist measures remain relatively rudimentary by international standards.

Ethnic and religious differences
Ethnic and religious conflicts provide breeding grounds for terrorist groups. Ethnic differences were significant factors generating the tensions that produced the coups in Fiji and the Solomons. While there are few Muslim communities in Oceania, the region adjoins Indonesia, the world's largest Muslim country. Fiji is alone in Oceania in having an important—around 8 per cent of the total population—Muslim community.

Surrogate targets
There are concerns that a weak state might provide a surrogate target for a terrorist group whose 'real' target was that country's larger friend or ally. These groups could be seeking to take advantage of the lower level of security in small states which rendered them 'soft' targets. It is likely that this risk will increase as more developed states increase their levels of antiterrorist security.

It was this fear of becoming a surrogate target that made several Pacific Island states wary of supporting the US-led war on Iraq, and concerned about the regional repercussions of Australia's direct involvement in the war. Australia's close identification with the US cause increased the terrorist threat to Australia and, by extension, the region. The prime minister of Papua New Guinea, Michael Somare, refused to back the US and warned that the Iraq conflict could 'rope' the region into a wider war.[7]

Platforms for attacks, unwilling hosts and transit points
There is also concern that an island state may 'unwittingly' become a transit point or a platform for a terrorist attack on a nearby country. The Melanesian 'arc of instability' presents this type of threat to Australia. Michael Somare,

reflecting on the terrorist threats, commented: 'Our proximity to Australia concerns us. It's only one hour's flight into Australian airspace.'[8]

Poor governance and failing states
Aid donors have become increasingly concerned that 'poor governance' will allow terrorism to flourish. This has resulted in a tougher approach to governance conditions on aid, and ultimately provided a major rationale for intervention into the 'failed state' of the Solomon Islands. But there is also concern that legitimate groups seeking political reform could be labelled terrorists. For instance, the Tongan Human Rights and Democracy Movement has expressed concern that the broad nature of the antiterrorism bill being promoted by the Tongan government could be used to suppress legitimate dissent.[9]

Failed or failing states are portrayed by New Zealand foreign minister, Phil Goff, as 'magnets' for terrorist groups, which can then establish 'footholds' in the region.[10] Goff further reflects: 'If states fail, this impacts on the well being of the people of those states and indirectly on the region. The vacuum of authority which results encourages international crime, including the smuggling of weapons and people.'[11] Australian prime minister John Howard has gone further and observed that 'failed states' in 'our region' jeopardise Australian security.[12]

Money laundering and other dubious financial activities
Money laundering by offshore banks operating in Pacific Island states, including Nauru, Cook Islands, Niue and the Marshall Islands, has been directly linked by the United States to the financing of terrorist and drug-trafficking activities. Passport sales by Pacific Island states, particularly Nauru, have also caused concern. So, too, has lax control of the shipping registries maintained by a number of Pacific Island states. For instance, al-Qaeda terrorists have used Tongan-registered ships.[13]

Under heavy pressure from the US, Australia and New Zealand, there have been significant moves by Pacific Island states to end these dubious financial activities. Nauru, the worst offender, has revoked all offshore banking licences.[14] The Cook Islands has made all the reforms necessary to be removed from the OECD's 'blacklist' of money launderers. Tonga has closed its shipping registry. Indeed the clampdown on money-laundering activities is one of the most significant developments for the Pacific region resulting from the war on terrorism.

Conclusion: Time for a Pacific Island peacekeeping force?

The Bali bombing and 9/11 have dramatically changed the way Australia views the Oceania region. Like its close ally the United States, it feels under threat from terrorism. The Australian-led Solomon Islands intervention force is clear evidence that the old 'hands-off' approach has been replaced by a 'get tough', proactive role in the region. The new security agenda for Australia includes armed intervention.

New Zealand does not share Australia's perception of the Pacific region as threatening. This can be explained partly by geography and culture. As an island state distant from the Asian continent, and with more than a fifth of its population Polynesian, New Zealand feels more relaxed about its Pacific environment. Its success in starting the process that brought peace to Bougainville demonstrated that it could make a difference for the better in the South Pacific. But the new Australian regional assertiveness means that New Zealand has been clearly relegated to second place. However, if Australia overplays its hand, and is considered to be acting more as a bully than a big brother, New Zealand's less assertive approach will be welcomed.

The Pacific Island states are affected by the post-9/11 security agendas of their aid donors, but have shown little interest in formulating their own responses to the threat posed by terrorism. Pressures to improve 'good governance' and end dubious financial practices, especially money laundering, have increased as a result of the war on terrorism. Pushed too far, this pressure could hasten the process of Pacific Island states tending to 'look north' to Asia where governance concerns are less pressing.

Participation by Pacific Island police and, where they exist, soldiers will be an important part of making a Solomon Islands-style, interventionist force respectable. But if such involvement is to move beyond tokenism, and island states are to develop a sense of ownership, it is important that the force be representative of the region and properly prepared for its role. The time is overdue for a Pacific Island peacekeeping force to be formed. As police-type work is mainly required, all the police forces of Pacific Forum states should be capable of making a contribution to the force. Those who have armies can contribute soldiers. It need not be a standing police and military force, as this would be too costly. A high state of readiness could be maintained through regular exercises. Deployment of the force should require the approval of the Pacific Island Forum. The alternative is appointing Australia as regional policeman—with New Zealand as its helper. This would not be in the interests of the region, or Australia, or New Zealand.

Notes

1. *Weekend Herald*, Christchurch, June 21–2 2003.
2. *Radio Australia*, 2 July 2003.
3. *ABC News*, 30 September 2003.
4. *Radio New Zealand International*, 10 June 2003.
5. *East–West Wire*, 19 March 2002.
6. *Cook Island News*, 3 October 2003.
7. *Pacnews*, 29 June 2003.
8. *Bulletin*, 29 April 2003, p.33.
9. *Pacific Island Report*, 31 October 2002.
10. *PINA*, 23 December 2002.
11. *Weekend Herald*, 21–2 June 2003, B16.
12. Radio New Zealand, *Morning Report*, 3 July 2003.
13. *Radio Australia*, 16 January 2003.
14. *Radio New Zealand International*, 14 June 2003.

7

NEW ZEALAND'S ROLE IN THE PACIFIC: THE NEW WARFARE STATE

Keith Suter

Introduction

Over a quarter of century of ago, Rod Alley got me interested in the issue of a South Pacific Nuclear Free Zone. The existing treaty is an example of how countries in the region can live by their hopes and not by their fears.

This chapter explores some options for New Zealand's role in the Pacific and deals with three groups of matters. First, it provides an overview of the changing nature of warfare over the past few thousand years. Second, it looks at the region's problems vis-à-vis globalisation and the new warfare state. Given that the Solomons is currently of so much concern, there is a case study of how the Solomons fits in with the broader issues of globalisation and failed states. Third, it concludes with some recommendations about how countries should adopt an alternative philosophy of international relations. If we do what we have always done, then we will get what we have always got—war. We need to think differently.

The changing nature of warfare

There are probably almost as many conflicts underway today as during the Cold War, but there is now a new warfare state: the conflicts are internal (not international) and guerrilla (rather than conventional). Peace has not broken out. Old tribal and ethnic disputes, which may have been frozen by the Cold War, have come back to life. Others have been on the boil for decades and, now that the United States (US) and the Soviet Union are not squabbling, they have suddenly come back into view. For example, the civil war in southern Sudan is one of Africa's oldest and bloodiest civil wars but it does not get much Western media coverage. The purpose of this section is to look at the changing nature of warfare.

First wave
There have been three main waves of warfare in recorded European history. First, there was guerrilla warfare. This required very little training. People (men, women and children) fought in a part-time capacity in small bands. Each person knew the rest of the group and so there was no need for a distinctive uniform. The weapons were often unsophisticated and based on everyday implements such as farming tools.

Then, for about the thousand years of the European Middle Ages, wars consisted of small battles (by modern standards) and sieges of fortified positions (especially castles). There were few full-time soldiers. Knights, for example, ran feudal estates as their main source of income and recruited their own farm workers as troops when required.

Second wave
The second wave of European warfare emerged around the seventeenth century. The nation-state system (which international lawyers date from 1648) meant that the basic unit of political power shifted from a small tribal area to the nation-state (or country), thereby giving rulers more people to tax and from whom to draw conscripts. The industrial revolution—which began in Britain in 1750—meant that industry could develop more destructive weapons, and fighting formations could be transported over longer distances. Europeans could now fight each other over colonies in the Americas, Africa and Asia.

The new form of warfare became so common that it acquired the title of 'conventional' warfare. Fighting formations became larger (and almost exclusively adult males) and it was necessary for all troops to have distinctive uniforms to distinguish them from the enemy. Armies also became more specialised in their work: they were to defend national security. This meant they were taken off the maintenance of law and order and that task was given to a separate force (the police).

Armies and navies became more professional. Defence personnel were set apart from the rest of the community; they lived in separate buildings and were controlled by legal codes usually more extensive than that of the civilian legal system. Restrictions were placed on civilian access to weapons—warfare became the exclusive right of the government. For the first time there were professional soldiers who spent large chunks of time without fighting. Previously personnel had been recruited for specific campaigns and then demobilised as soon as the fighting stopped.

Now personnel were in permanent employment but fighting only took up part of their time.

During the first half of the twentieth century, the nature of conventional warfare changed again.[1] It used to be about humans killing humans. Beginning in World War I, land warfare became far more mechanised. Warfare became a matter of machines killing machines. The last Allied cavalry charge was on 8 November 1917, when units of the Canadian army defeated a German cavalry regiment. There were few horses used at all in World War II. In 1941, the United Kingdom had 100,000 vehicles in the Middle East. By the time of D-Day in June 1944, there was one vehicle for every 4.77 allied soldiers. Between 1939 and 1945, 130,000 aircraft were produced in the United Kingdom. In addition, 119,000 German aircraft and 303,000 American aircraft were built. Warfare had become an activity of quartermasters general and production planners. Generals were more like corporate chief executive officers.

The 'tail' became bigger than the 'teeth'. In order to keep one soldier at the front, there were six persons drawn from such civilian occupations as catering, engineering, medicine, building, transportation and law. Each arm of service became a society within a society.

World War II will likely remain the world's largest conventional war. Other wars have been longer (notably the Iran–Iraq war of the 1980s), but none is likely to be as extensive, intensive and expensive. For example, we have just been celebrating the 60th anniversary of the Battle of Kursk (July 1943), which was the largest battle in world history—involving four million Soviet and German troops—and also the largest tank battle.[2] There is not likely to be another battle bigger than Kursk.

The prime factor in the decline of conventional warfare is the cost of the mechanisation of warfare. Governments cannot afford the same stock of equipment as they used to acquire. Humans were comparatively cheap—they often came via conscription. But machines are expensive both to purchase and to maintain. The US B2 bomber, at US$2.2 billion each, is said to cost three times its weight in gold. The machines are also much more destructive: they travel further with more firepower than previous weapons. Machines can also be destroyed at a faster rate, however, with less chance of their ever being repaired.

All major conventional wars since the early 1960s, which have resulted in a clear victory, have been won in less than six weeks. If one side cannot defeat the other in that time, then the war is likely to drag on, such as the inconclusive Iran–Iraq war, which ran for eight years. The crucial six-week period is because of the limitations of equipment and supply: governments can no longer afford large reserves of equipment.

Third wave

Meanwhile, guerrilla warfare—the third wave of warfare—has grown rapidly since World War II. Every conflict underway today involves guerrillas in at least one party to the conflict. Guerrilla warfare turns conventional warfare's reasoning upside down. Guerrilla warfare is essentially political—it is about winning the hearts and minds of people. It is not so much about taking and holding a set piece of territory.

Guerrillas do not need a large amount of firepower to do this because they are only carrying out sporadic raids. Too much firepower, as with the US troops in Vietnam, can alienate the local population since there is a temptation to use it wantonly. The US did not lose in Vietnam because of a shortage of firepower but partly because of the excessive use of it.[3] They turned potential supporters away because the excessive use of force resulted in the death of innocent civilians (a mistake the Americans are now trying to avoid in Iraq).

Guerrillas can lose battle after battle and yet still win the war because guerrilla warfare is a form of attrition. There is a wearing down of the conventional forces until exhaustion and frustration set in.

As modern life has become more sophisticated, so has it become more vulnerable to disruption by guerrilla groups. A century and a half ago, for example, homes in New Zealand, Australia, Britain or the United States had to look after their own water supply—and so each household was far more self-reliant than it is today with such widespread dependence on centralised reticulation systems. A guerrilla group could now disrupt a town's water supply, similarly, electricity is also centrally supplied.

Modern life in large cities is one of anonymity. People living next door to each other often know little about each other. A guerrilla group could operate from a city district and the neighbours would not know it (as the British army found in Northern Ireland and the Israelis continue to find in the Holy Land). This anonymity makes it difficult for the military to get information. Guerrillas can melt away in the crowd, like fish in a sea—as the Americans found in Iraq after April 2003. This also helps explain the problems the US has had in finding Osama bin Laden in southern Afghanistan/northern Pakistan.

To conclude, the new warfare state presents many new challenges to traditional military and political thinking. The situation is even more complicated when globalisation is taken into consideration.

Globalisation

The largest military operation in the South Pacific since World War II is now underway. An Australian-led regional force has intervened in the Solomons Islands (at the invitation of the national parliament). This may be the beginning of a new era because Australia and New Zealand have previously resisted all calls for military intervention in the region's upheavals.

There is now greater official recognition that many of the South Pacific countries are close to becoming 'failed states' (the Solomons being the region's first). That there should be any discussion of such a crisis seems unusual. After all, the region was so pro-American in the Cold War that the Soviet Union and China made very few attempts to export any tensions there. It was one of the few areas of the world that was largely bypassed by direct Cold War confrontations. It was an 'American lake'.[4] The region is potentially wealthy, not least from the sea and tourism. The countries are separated by large expances of water and so unlike (say) in Africa, there can be no mass migrations to the South Pacific of people fleeing conflicts in Africa or Asia.[5] All of the states have links with Western developed countries and have received much aid from them. Indeed, on a per capita basis, more aid has probably gone to this region than to any other region in the world. Nonetheless, not one country can be held up as a sparkling success story of decolonisation.

What has gone wrong? The essence of the problem, I suggest, is globalisation. The world is moving from an era when national boundaries were very important, to one where they are not. 'Globalisation' for me refers to the declining power of national governments generally. This is more than just economics. It is how the world is being ordered. An entire era is passing away.[6]

National governments are a comparatively new idea. International lawyers date them from 1648: the end of the Thirty Years War in Europe and the Treaty of Westphalia (hence the name of the present world order: 'Westphalian system'). Prior to that people in Europe lived in small tribes, possibly as part of a large empire, or in city-states. There were few countries as we know them today.

No one suddenly decided in 1648 to create the Westphalian system. It was only with the benefit of hindsight that people could see that a new world order had been created as a result of the breaking up of the Holy Roman Empire. Peoples ('nations') were now to be governed by 'states', hence the title of nation-states (as distinct from, say, the previous city-states). As the Europeans colonised the world, so they took this system with them. The newly independent colonies based themselves on the nation-state system (for example, in Africa where about 55 nation-states have been imposed on a patchwork quilt of about 200 major tribes). The United Nations currently has 191 nation-state members, with East Timor as the newest.

The nation-state system is now so prevalent that it is seen as the norm in world politics. It has worn well but now it is wearing out. National governments are no longer so relevant to world politics. Instead, they are having to share their power in three ways.

Economic globalisation
Economic globalisation is being driven by transnational corporations, which are now the major player in world economics. They, rather than national governments, set the pace of economic change.[7] The antiglobalisation demonstrators are right to identify the problems that some corporations create, such as the exploitation of labour (including child labour), the manipulation of national taxation regimes to avoid paying tax, and the destruction of the environment. Transnational corporations can also play havoc with foreign currency transactions. For example, American banker Andy Krieger was one of the legendary foreign currency speculators in the late 1980s. He speculated particularly on the New Zealand dollar (the 'Kiwi'). On one occasion he sold roughly the entire money supply of New Zealand. New Zealand finance officials privately told him that they did not mind him driving down the price of the Kiwi because it would make exports cheaper and spur economic growth. In other words, this 25-year-old trader could do what the government could not—drive down the Kiwi's value and force economic change on a lethargic business community.[8]

But it is worth noting that the corporations are responding to consumer demand. They make available what people want to buy. They may stimulate consumer demand but they do not create it. Many people with money have opted for a consumption-driven lifestyle. In doing so they are exercising their free will. As the *Economist* magazine has pointed out, 'McDonald's does not march people into its outlets at the point of a gun. Nike does not require people to wear its trainers on pain of imprisonment. If people buy those things, it is because they choose to, not because globalisation is forcing them.'[9]

In addition, while many people in developing countries do have appalling lives working in factories, no country has yet found a smooth way to move from an agricultural society to an industrial one. The British suffered from the industrial revolution in the nineteenth century; now it is the turn of many Asian countries. Besides, current life on a peasant farm is very harsh and should not be romanticised—hence the attraction of the bright lights of the cities.

Popular globalisation
But the globalisation trend has some positive developments.[10] A second form of globalisation consists of 'people power' movements (non-governmental organisations or civil society organisations). These are a way for ordinary people to work together for a better world. Their members are disenchanted with politicians because they have such little power. Therefore the people have decided to set their own agenda. Examples include Amnesty International, Greenpeace, and World Vision.

Ironically, some of the opponents of globalisation use the products of globalisation to oppose economic globalisation, like their use of cyberspace, and elaborate websites. They also know how to use the international mass media to play to a global audience and how to tap into the growing worries that people in many countries have about economic globalisation. All of these events are feats worthy of the massive advertising budgets of transnational corporations, like Coca-Cola or McDonalds. But they are all done cheaply via the Internet, email, word of mouth, and graffiti.

Public order globalisation
The final example of globalisation is 'public order globalisation'. There are no national solutions to transnational problems. Pollution, diseases, and changes in weather patterns are all examples of a country's inability to solve its problems on its own. A country may have a fine record in environmental protection, for example, but this is of little value if it is living downwind of a dirty country. Similarly global diseases are not new (for example, the Plague destroyed about one-third of Europe between 1348 and 1350).

What is new is the speed with which a virus can move around the world. Thanks to aviation, a virus is only thirty-six hours at most from every other part of the globe.

Therefore governments have to work together, not because they like to do so but because they have little choice. They either work together or perish separately. Until the recent expansion of the United Nations (UN) peacekeeping operations, about 80 per cent of the UN's money went on economic and social cooperation. This work is done by the UN everyday, all day, via specialised bodies such as the World Health Organisation, the UN Environment Programme, the International Maritime Organisation and the UN Children's Fund. If the UN disappeared today, it would be necessary to invent it to do these basic tasks that we take for granted.

This is called functional cooperation: getting experts to work together out of the public eye.[11] The other type of international cooperation is political cooperation. But this is often hampered because politicians like to approach every issue with an open mouth (such as the current negotiations over the Middle East). But technicians can and do get together for functional cooperation purposes and they gradually knit the world together into a system of mutually beneficial arrangements, such as the standardisation of telephone systems and the exchange of information on diseases and weather. This is not exciting work and it is usually ignored by the mass media—but this is what improves the daily life of many people.

The South Pacific's problems in coping with globalisation

First, almost all the countries are microstates and have some difficulty coping with the requirements of international law and international politics. There are nineteen of these entities in the region, ranging in population from 5.2 million in Papua New Guinea to 1000 in Tokelau. This list includes French Polynesia and New Caledonia, which are still territories of metropolitan France and which may eventually become independent. There are other territories, in addition, such as Pitcairn Island (a British dependency with less than one hundred people, who are descendants of sailors from the wreck of Captain Bligh's ship *Bounty*) and American Samoa (which is now effectively part of the United States).

Twelve of these nineteen entities are in the United Nations. They total seven million or so people, out of a total world population of six billion, and they constitute about 6 per cent of the UN's total of member-states. It is a great financial burden being represented by professional diplomats at international gatherings, let alone maintaining all the other trappings of national status, such as national airlines and military forces. It is like a poor person determined to belong to an expensive exclusive Wellington club.

Second, a related issue is constitutional colonialism. The outgoing imperial powers left elaborate national constitutions based on centuries of their own evolving democratic traditions. Many of these documents have run into trouble. They are not applicable to the local political cultures. This is not to pass a value judgment on the worth of the pre-existing South Pacific political traditions. It is simply to recognise that these traditions are different and that it is an error to try to graft Western constitutions onto different political cultures. There has often been little sense of local ownership of the constitutions as a consequence.

A related issue is educational colonialism. Teachers teach what they were once taught. The outgoing colonial powers failed to provide education that would be a suitable preparation for independence as a country in the South Pacific. Perhaps the educators did not themselves know what would be required and so were guided by what they did back in their metropolitan countries. After all, these countries had all had spirited national debates over what was relevant for their own peoples. If they disagreed about what was right for their home populations, they could hardly be expected to know what was relevant for colonised peoples.

Third, since 1970, the South Pacific has received about US$50 billion in foreign aid. But there is little 'development' to show for it. Part of the problem is that aid now tends to be given to assist the donor rather than the recipient. Most aid is tied and bilateral, rather than the untied aid given through multilateral aid organisations, such as the United Nations. For example, most of Australia's foreign aid never leaves Australia. Some of it goes to Australian universities to educate students from the South Pacific.

In May 2003 an article by the Australian academic (and former World Bank economist) Helen Hughes triggered a new debate.[12] In the article she is critical of foreign aid programmes and has recommended that they be stopped to the South Pacific because the money is used there for corrupt purposes and breeds a culture of dependency. Debate centred particularly on her claim that the system of common land holdings has hindered the creation of an entrepreneurial culture. The South Pacific way of life has made anthropology a local growth industry for Westerners (such as Margaret Mead). The foreigners come from cultures based on greed, the Protestant work ethic, and individual enterprise, and they have tended to see the South Pacific way of life as having many attractive alternative features. But Hughes has argued that 'not one country in the world has developed on the basis of communal land ownership'.[13] She has also argued that 'clan loyalty, admirable in traditional societies, is inappropriate for a high income modern society . . . Clan loyalty makes it impossible for individuals to save and invest.'[14]

Meanwhile, aimless, unemployed youths drift out of the decaying, suffocating villages into the cities (which tend to be the more important recipients of foreign aid). They have little scope for employment and drift into crime and drug use, and contract sexual diseases such as HIV/AIDS. Much of the violence in South Pacific countries (such as in the Solomons, and in Papua New Guinea's troubled capital city, Port Moresby) comes from crime rather than some clear political agenda. There is an undertone of frustration and racism that derives from unemployment and resentment of the wealth of others rather than a political ideology of any sort. Communists and Islamic fanatics cannot be blamed for any of this.

Additionally, economic decline feeds upon itself. Unstable countries lose a major source of foreign tourist income. After the first coup in Fiji in 1987, the Solomon Islands ran an advertising campaign in Australian travel magazines, saying: 'Come to the Solomons, the fighting ended here in 1945.' Nowadays, tourists do not go to the Solomons, either.

To conclude, the outlook is likely to get worse rather than better. First, the Australian and New Zealand governments have had no great enthusiasm for the intervention in the Solomons. Their involvement has been largely due to 9/11 and the fear that the Solomons, as a failed state, could eventually become a host to international terrorist groups. While this may not have happened, it is clearly the reasoning of the Australian prime minister, John Howard. Australians have rallied behind the operation because in the main they like to rally behind their defence forces. The mood could have turned sour if Australian soldiers had been killed, and there were fears of an emerging 'Vietnam'-type quagmire. Australians are not generally interested in South Pacific military adventures, and they have no imperial aspirations—they do not want their government making a habit of these South Pacific ventures, and they are not interested in Australia becoming the regional sheriff.

Second, it seems that the domestic situation in many South Pacific countries will get even worse. For example, adult-onset diabetes is increasingly the main health problem in the region. Nauru has one of the world's worst rates (coequal with some American First Nations in Arizona). South Pacific Islanders are becoming more sedentary, and are eating more sugary Western foodstuffs and less traditional foods than their forebears. Their genetic inheritance has equipped them to survive food shortages by storing fat on their bodies, but not to cope with a flood of sugar and diary fats. All the national healthcare systems have enough challenges coping with existing health problems. The diabetes epidemic will overwhelm these systems (with the need they generate for surgical operations and with the shortage of rehabilitation staff).

Finally, there is growing speculation that global climate change will increase the South Pacific's vulnerability to environmental problems. Rising sea levels are engulfing parts of some countries. This rise is the result of the melting of the polar ice caps and the fact that warm water expands. A country does not need to be inundated to be uninhabitable. Rising sea levels bring salt water into areas that are used for cultivation. Tuvalu's 11,000 citizens may become the world's first country to claim that they are all 'environmental refugees' and seek asylum in Australia or New Zealand.

To conclude, the regional intervention force in the Solomons is only the tip of the South Pacific national insecurity iceberg. The region has many problems, not least the fact that so few countries outside the region are concerned about its fate.

The Solomons as a failed state[15]

The crisis in the Solomons may be seen, I suggest, as a case study of the problems of coping with globalisation and the weaknesses in the nation-state system. First, many of the problems in the South Pacific are legacies from the era of European colonialism. The European impact will long be felt in the South Pacific. Eighty per cent of the current national borders in the world were created by Europeans. Similarly, most of the nation-states in the South Pacific were created by Europeans without heed to local history or culture. The Solomons have been inhabited for about 3000 years. The first Europeans to arrive there were the Spanish in the sixteenth century. They had been sent from their colony in Peru to look for the fabled 'lost isles' of King Solomon, reputed to be full of gold and silver. Ironically, there is some gold in the islands, but there is far more wealth in the sea from fish, palm oil, timber reserves, and foreign tourism. If the country had been able to develop economically, it could be quite wealthy in South Pacific terms.

The South Pacific colonies were exploited by 'mercenaries, missionaries and misfits'.[16] The Solomons certainly had its share of the first two. In the late nineteenth century the islands were raided by mercenaries known as 'blackbirders' who captured labourers to work on the plantations in Queensland and Fiji. A total of about 30,000 Solomon Islanders are believed to have been taken to these foreign lands between 1870 and 1911. The British government established a protectorate on the main islands in 1893 to try to stop this forced labour. Other islands were taken over between 1898 and 1899. A group of separate islands therefore found themselves subjects of the British Queen in the same colony.

The missionaries were also busy in the islands. The Solomons is a strongly Christian country, where visitors will be asked for details of their Christian denomination in much the same way that New Zealanders or Australians will talk about which sporting teams they support. The churches are full and very active. They provide a range of welfare services.

The British did little to prepare the country for independence. After World War II (in which the Solomons suffered a great deal) the British were anxious to get out of all their colonies as quickly as possible and with as little expenditure as necessary. The Solomons became independent of Britain in 1978, though the Queen remains the head of state. The country has a population of about 450,000, with English as the national language (though there are sixty-eight other languages still spoken across the islands). In 2000, the then prime minister, Bartholomew Ulafa'alu, noted that the: 'Solomon Islands is a melting pot of different races. In the west, we are close to the Australian Aborigines. In the east, we are Malay; in the north, Melanesian; and in the south, Tongan. We are united because of external power. [It was] the imposition of unity. History shows ethnic tensions in post-British societies because the development [under the British] was not deeply rooted, not equally distributed . . . It was networks of cronies in power that held countries together.'[17]

Second, there are the problems of poor economic development. The South Pacific's problems are not just ethnic. Racial labels are often used for political purposes. Economic growth is the glue that now holds societies together. A lack of economic growth means a lack of glue. All the South Pacific countries have pockets of poverty, some worse than others. In all previous centuries, people were poor but did not know it because they had no external frame of reference. Now, thanks to economic globalisation, radio and television have brought the world into their villages, and they can compare their plight with that of people who live well elsewhere. Similarly, they can compare their lives with those of the foreign tourists who visit their countries.

Many of the Western-style economic development formulae over the past three decades have not worked. Governments have encouraged people to move into cash crops, companies to borrow from overseas banks, and foreign companies to invest. They have done what the textbooks have laid down. Western consultants have done well in selling advice but the countries have not necessarily done well in buying it.

Meanwhile, there are unemployment problems in Australia and New Zealand and so there are tighter immigration restrictions. This means that there are not the same opportunities for South Pacific Islanders to work overseas temporarily, with the hope of sending money back home.

Overshadowing these developments is the unequal struggle between small island governments and transnational corporations. The latter can play governments off against each other in the search for resources and manufacturing locations. They can bribe local politicians and manipulate the local media (for example, through the purchasing power of advertisements). They can also recruit local opinion formers and business leaders to be their advocates. Economic globalisation has proceeded so quickly that government leaders have been blind-sided by change and caught by surprise. Various people (including myself) have written on this process for many years. But the politicians and their officials have not paid attention and now it is probably too late to reverse economic globalisation. They need to find ways of making the most of the new era—and they seem equally unsuccessful in that.

Third, there is the problem of weak states and the need for strong leaders. A developed country has a weak leader and a strong state. In other words, the New Zealand, British or Australian prime minister can go overseas, and the country will continue to run much as before in their absence. There will be no military coup, government salaries will be paid, and trains will run. Many apolitical citizens may not even notice or care about the temporary absence of their leader.

In many developing countries, however, there is a weak state and a strong leader. In other words, the death of a leader may see major changes occur because the state is so dependent on the leader setting the sense of national direction. A problem for the South Pacific is the lack of strong states. There are problems of corruption, lack of transparency and lack of stability. The culture of democracy in developed countries did not develop overnight; it evolved after many decades, if not centuries, of trial and error. Developing countries have not had long enough to develop their own culture of democracy.

In short, the fear among some Australian commentators is that the intervention in the Solomons really is the beginning of a new era. Many of the issues in the Solomons are systemic in the region. For example, all the countries have borders imposed by European colonialists to suit their map-making ambitions rather than to accommodate ethnic groups. They have small domestic markets, a narrow resource and production base, high unit costs for infrastructure, heavy dependence on external trade, and they are vulnerable to environmental disasters such as cyclones. The July 2003 intervention could be simply the beginning of an era in which more and more operations are required.

Disarming militia groups and restoring law and order are difficult enough. Trying to rebuild—or build for the first time—economic and social infrastructure will be even more difficult. As the postcolonial experiences in Africa and Asia have shown, there is no standard formula for economic and social growth.

Recommendations

First, it is necessary to acknowledge that this is a new era that requires new ways of thinking. The old formulae will not necessarily work. For example, this chapter has argued that guerrilla warfare is the major form of warfare in the future. But this is not reflected in the conventional-warfare bias in defence expenditure. Much more money should go into training for guerrilla operations and UN peacekeeping operations (such as the expansion of the Australian Defence Force Peacekeeping Centre, at Newcastle). Meanwhile, I am doubtful about Australia's need to purchase new tanks. They are more a prestige item for the Army than a necessary tool for the new warfare state.

Second, Australia has signed up for the US National Missile Defense programme. This is also a waste of money. Even the conservative Australian newspaper the *Australian Financial Review* has expressed reservations: 'The idea of destroying missiles before they can do any damage is attractive. But it is also far-fetched and risky. The [Australian] government hasn't made out a compelling case for climbing aboard, or if it has, it hasn't bothered to share it with us.'[18]

Third, countries should have a foreign policy philosophy that requires a new approach to settling problems. It should be based on what unites countries, rather than on what divides them, namely, public order globalisation. This includes the need to work together through the United Nations to promote economic development, to protect the environment (for instance, ratifying the Kyoto Protocol on climate change) and to promote human rights.

Fourth, there should also be increased foreign aid. The UN target (which is met by only four of the twenty-two developed countries) is 0.7 per cent of gross national product (GNP). Australia is one of those that have got meaner as they have got richer. It is well away from the UN foreign aid target. Additionally, the aid should be 'untied' and put through multilateral agencies and non-governmental organisations (rather than kept in Australia and handed out to businesses and universities).[19]

The usual question is: where will all the money come from? Well, when we want to find the money, we can do so. It is a matter of having the right priorities. We can find money for war—we should be able to find money for peace. After all, preventing conflict from breaking out is, in the long run, a lot cheaper than actually having to fight conflicts.

Notes

1   See Keith Suter, 'From Boer War to East Timor: Warfare in the 20th Century', *Contemporary Review* (December 1999), pp.287–93.
2   See Karl Heinz-Frieser et al, 'Kursk—Sixty Years On', *Journal of the Royal United Services Institute* (October 2003), pp.78–89.
3   For example, in 1974 I interviewed some of the survivors of the My Lai massacre in South Vietnam. The survivors had little sympathy for the National Liberation Front/Viet Cong. But at least the NLF/VC were restrained in their use of violence because they had so little ammunition. They had to make the most of it. This was not a problem for the Americans, who occasionally fired weapons just out of boredom.
4   The phrase comes from Peter Hayes et al, *American Lake: How the Nuclear Build Up in the Cause of 'Peace' Fuels the Threat of War* (London, Penguin, 1986).
5   The only South Pacific country with a large enough population to have a 'mass' movement of people is Papua New Guinea. The only other potential mass movement (though strictly outside the South Pacific region) is a Chinese exodus from Indonesia south into Australia, if there were again anti-Chinese riots amid civil unrest. In 1965–96 the Chinese fled north into Singapore/Malaysia. The Australian Government is evidently counting on them going in that direction again if Indonesia falls into chaos and people pick on the minority of rich Chinese as scapegoats.

6   See Keith Suter, *Global Order and Global Disorder: Globalization and the Nation-State* (Westport, CT, Praeger, 2003).
7   See Keith Suter, *Global Agenda: Economics, the Environment and the Nation-State* (Sydney, Albatross, 1995).
8   Frank Partnoy, *Infectious Greed: How Deceit and Risk Corrupted the Financial Markets* (London, Profile Books, 2003), pp.19–24.
9   'Is Globalization Doomed?' *Economist*, 29 September 2001, p.13.
10 See Keith Suter, *In Defence of Globalization* (Kensington, University of New South Wales Press, 2000).
11 See David Mitrany, *The Functional Theory of Politics* (London, Martin Robertson, 1975).
12 Helen Hughes, 'Aid Has Failed the Pacific', *Issue Analysis* 33 (Sydney, Centre for Independent Studies, 2003).
13 Hughes, 'Aid Has Failed the Pacific', p.11.
14 Hughes, 'Aid Has Failed the Pacific', p.12.
15 For an introduction, see Elsina Wainwright et al, *Our Failing Neighbour: Australia and the Future of the Solomon Islands* (Canberra, Australian Strategic Policy Institute, 2003).
16 Rowan Callick, 'Papua New Guinea and the Pacific' in Stephen Mills (ed), *Asian Business Insight* (Sydney, Financial Review Library, 1995), p.246.
17 Bartholomew Ulufa'alu, quoted in Jean Ker Walsh, 'The Region's Crunch Time', *Eureka Street*, 10, 6 (2000), p.14.
18 'Missile Plan Needs Proper Appraisal', *Australian Financial Review*, 6 (2003), p.70.
19 Australian politician Pauline Hanson, in the late 1990s, triggered a national debate over the value of foreign aid. She complained that the money was being sent overseas (which was the case in the 1960s and 1970s). This was now a quaint view because (as noted above) most of it stays in Australia and goes into Australian businesses (including universities). The government was eventually forced to reply to her complaints and defend foreign aid. It was pressured into doing so by the Australian business community (which lobbied the government via the deputy prime minister, who was the minister for trade). The business community does well out of foreign aid, and it did not want Ms Hanson, with her 1960s perception of foreign aid, ruining the support it receives from the government.

8

THE CONCEPT OF THE 'FAILED STATE': A BROBDINGNAGIAN VIEW FROM LILLIPUT

Richard Herr

Introduction

A concept of the 'failed state'—a post-Cold War era notion—has appeared in the South Pacific and quickly gained some popular currency in recent years. The term is used freely in the media as something that the lay reader will understand both for what it denotes and connotes. The value of the term is yet to be established, however, and I will argue it poses real risks for Australian and New Zealand relationships with their Island neighbours if the concept is not used carefully and with discretion. The problem with too facile a usage of the term is that of any stereotype—it seems to convey a simple meaning that most can understand but, in fact, it is simplistic to a dangerous degree. The risks are particularly high for the Pacific Island countries (PICs) since most are microstates and thus especially subject to the asymmetry of power and changes in the rules governing the comity of nations.

If failed state is to have any substantive meaning for international relations or in the study of international relations, it will have to inform and influence relationships within the comity of nations. Of course, the formal meaning or impact of a new category for identifying state actors will not prevent the governmental and academic spin doctors from using it as an emotional lever to sway public opinion. However, if this term is to have practical content, the 'spin' will have to take into account some contact with real world politics. The literature on failed states has burgeoned over the past decade or so but to date there is no more than a modicum of agreement on either the meaning or the expected consequences of this concept. Contested language is the 'meat and potatoes' of diplomacy so this dispute is scarcely surprising especially where new concepts are being developed. However, as will be discussed below, there is one area where views have converged on the use of the term failed state. This is that it demands action from the international community to intervene in these states.[1]

This action ought to be part of, and consistent with, the general practice of international relations. I do not believe this consistency is being pursued (much less recognised) at present because, as will be developed later, there is a fundamental cleavage separating two camps on its use. Nevertheless, it seems to me there is a broader theme underlying the development of the concept of the failed state. This notion is connected with other terms that have come into vogue in recent years as well such as the 'rogue state'. The leading states in the international community in the post-Cold War era have attempted to rewrite the book on state responsibility in the wake of earlier temporising during the Cold War. Central to this revision has been increased pressure on weaker states to meet standards of responsibility not required previously. For a state to 'fail', it must have lapsed in some significant area of state responsibility just as for a state to be a 'rogue' it must be operating contrary to the standards expected of it as a state in the international arena.[2]

The duality of sovereignty and changing standards for state responsibility

The problem of identifying precisely the appropriate standards for state responsibility stems from the origins of the modern state system. The legitimisation and formalisation of the state system in Europe through the Peace of Westphalia in 1648 set in train an evolving arrangement for managing international order based on the centrality of the principle of sovereignty. Sovereignty was itself a highly contested term then (as it is today) being variously regarded as either the highest law-making authority or the most effective law enforcement power.[3] The clash of definitions has had a profound effect on modern attempts to explain international order but, from the beginning, both definitions were agreed that there was a clear and almost sacred boundary that divided one polity from another. The recognition of an international frontier established two separate but interdependent notions of order. There is an internal order, which rests on the state and its relationship with its people, and there is an external order that is managed (or created) by the relations amongst states.

These two orders are essential one to the other in the modern period as the state system has become entrenched around the world. However, their relationship was not always seen as linked. The political pendulum has swung between giving pride of place to one or the other view of order. Initially, this sovereignty challenged and then fractured the international order centred on the primacy of the Church in Rome and replaced it with an order based in local control. Over the centuries since, the duality of sovereignty has swung to emphasising international priorities and then back to domestic concerns. The twentieth century exhibited both ends of this dialectic. Following World War I, the European powers agreed to redraw the map of Europe to match nationality with statehood on the logic that, if nationality legitimated the state, there would be fewer international disputes generated by internally divided states. The same logic was extended to the international empires globally after World War II. As the winds of change swept across Asia, Africa, the Caribbean and into the Pacific, ever smaller units had their sovereignty restored and they entered the comity of nations. However, by the end of the century, concern for the external order amongst states reasserted itself as a priority in the wake of the collapse of the Cold War and so gave rise to a new emphasis on state responsibility.

A number of factors contributed to the process of decolonisation based in nationality throughout the second half of the twentieth century. Undoubtedly, however, the ideological rivalry of the Cold War fuelled the willingness of many to turn a blind eye to the consequences for international order of pressing nationality to its limits. The process took on a life of its own, especially through the United Nations(UN), and was pursued so vigorously that decolonisation became an end in itself. Many new states were states in name only—lacking either the legitimacy of nationality or the capacity to contribute effectively to international order, either by maintaining internal stability or by meeting external obligations. These are the polities that Robert H. Jackson has grouped together under the rubric of 'quasi-states'.[4]

The mitigation strategy of 'nation building' was invented and embraced (often without any visible warmth) to address the international community's suppressed qualms on the proliferation of 'quasi-states'. Arguably, the consensus of support for decolonisation, and the repeated practical attempts through the United Nations to promote it, created an implied contract between the 'quasi-states' and the international community. The responsibility for this implied contract rested formally with the UN's membership, individually and collectively, but all too often these states left the implementation of nation building to the world body and its various agencies. Whether the commitment to nation building was ever fully honoured by the international community (or its institutional agents) will be debated in the future as it has been in the past. Nevertheless, the extent of the international community's responsibility for the states created under the rush to decolonise has real implications for what kind of obligations exist under international norms to shore up 'quasi-states' in the face of looming failure. Some, such as Gareth Evans, believe these obligations are real and so justified (and even compelled) international humanitarian intervention.[5] Even Kofi Annan, secretary general of the United Nations, argued in 1999 that there was a humanitarian obligation on UN members to intervene even when the UN itself was unable to agree on intervention to prevent the worst consequences of state failure.[6]

Such views have contrasted markedly with the views of the current administration in Washington whose neoconservative agenda has interpreted (some) weak states more as threats than as objects for international compassion. Particularly since 9/11, ineffective states are seen as locations for terrorist threats against Western interests. However, even as it came to office, the George W. Bush regime asserted a right to pre-emptive strikes against those whose standards of sovereign responsibility were deficient in directions that appeared to threaten the United States administration. Initially the perceived threat was from 'rogue states' and so assumed to be within traditional Realist power politics (being pressure exerted by one state against another). The tragedy of the September 2001 terrorist attacks in the US refocused awareness away from states pursuing aberrant external policies to states so lacking in internal authority that non-state actors could use their territory to threaten effective states elsewhere. The reinvention of gunboat diplomacy as a doctrine of pre-emptive strikes has transformed the original objectives for developing a category of failed state.

The concept of the failed state today

As a consequence of such developments, the concept of the failed state has become a bone caught in a struggle between two contending schools of thought on the consequences of failed states for the rest of the world. On the one hand, there are those who initially developed the concept to use as a diagnostic tool to perform a political triage to identify and save the neediest of the states losing the struggle to cope with sovereignty.[7] On the other, are those who, more recently, would use the concept to identify states whose collapse would constitute a serious contagion threatening international order and would need to be contained, or quarantined in some political sense, for the security of other members of the international community. The imagery of a political triage seeks external (humanitarian) intervention in order to save ineffective states from collapse by addressing their domestic needs. The Bush approach, embraced and supported by conservative allies abroad, sees power as a means of removing infectious risks to the international body politic.

The latter interpretation not only argues for a different form of intervention than the triage approach but it also undermines a collective response to dealing with the problems of the so-called failed states. The notion of state failure as an infectious contagion shifts the burden for action (in international state practice terms) from the international community as a body to older, power-based usages that favour individual action. In short, as with gunboat diplomacy in previous centuries, breaches of international norms will be addressed by the powerful, that is, those states with the capacity to pursue redress for perceived grievances. Unilateralism is encouraged by this interpretation of state responsibility not solely because of the legitimisation of military power but also as a right of redress—even in anticipation of a possible danger. The recent sophistry in the justification for the 'coalition of the willing' in acting against Iraq illustrates this distortion in international law. The alleged immediate threat of weapons of mass destruction (WMD) gave a plausible, if transparently inadequate, case in law for invoking self-defence as a basis for war. The real objective—regime change—could not be used and the more aware and sensitive policy makers in the George W. Bush administration such as Secretary of State Colin Powell recognised this and so argued for the WMD rationale both within the White House and at the United Nations.

It is true that international order is not regulated by the same rules that govern domestic relations. However, when looking to ways of improving international order, especially in the direction of making it more lawful, looking at the principles of municipal law is not a bad place to start. One pertinent tenet is that of *nemo judex in parte sua*. It is a fundamental principle of natural justice which states that no person can judge a case in which he or she is party. This is not an easy value to implement internationally since the principle of 'self-help' is not only deeply ingrained; there is often little substitute for it. Nevertheless, the growth and development of the international justice system makes it increasingly less desirable that states contrive excuses to violate this basic legal principle. Allying the concept of the pre-emptive strike to that of the failed state as a type of international free-fire zone is an enormously retrograde step from developing effective international standards for state responsibility.

Implications of the failed states for South Pacific microstates

There are many specific reasons why the general concept of the failed state is inappropriate in the Pacific Islands. The first and most significant is that the nearly universal condition of being microstates could be seen as condemning them to being failed states, at least by one definition of this term. Gerald Helman and Steven Ratner described the failed state as one 'utterly incapable of sustaining itself as a member of the international community'.[8] How precisely one is to assess 'utterly' is open to question but their definition draws attention to the need for states to be self-sustaining. This was an international norm until the twentieth century but, as noted above, it was relaxed then to permit the dismantling of empires. Thus, the 'small power' was a category of state that was able to look after itself but could not enjoy an extensive engagement in international affairs. The advent of a category of state—the microstate—below that of a small power suggests a category of statehood where the state is substantially dependent on the support of a favourable international climate to maintain its existence. And, if that climate changes, as it has since the end of the Cold War, earlier guarantees of survival may be called into question.

I am not trying to create a straw man argument here based on the semantic inelegance associated with the definition of failed states. However, I do want to draw attention to the way that any significant level of state incapacity can give grounds for being labelled a failed state. The difficulties that all Pacific microstates encounter in coping with statehood are often similar whether they might be 'quasi-states' grappling with the challenges of nation building or established polities such as Nauru, Samoa or Tonga that approximated the ideal of a 'nation' well before the arrival of Europeans with their notions of the state. Of course, the distinction between and amongst the PICs as nations and their varying capacities to cope with statehood has been complicated by a certain 'roguishness' in some quarters. Those PICs that have pursued more adventurous approaches to the use of their rights as sovereign entities are perceived as posing threats to other states not because they were 'failing' to meet expected standards of internal order. Rather, lax offshore banking laws that allowed massive money laundering and tax haven opportunities, a willingness to auction their nationality without due care by selling passports, registering flags of convenience and the like have had little to do with state incapacity. The contemporary paranoia over all forms of non-state threats to established states have appeared to intensify some concerns for the state incapacity of Pacific microstates, especially in Australia.

When Prime Minister John Howard invited his Solomon Islands counterpart, Sir Allan Kemakeza, to visit Canberra in June 2003 to discuss Australian intervention in the strife-torn neighbour, the issue of a failed state was not formally raised. Ostensibly, their talks were based on a renewed appreciation for the deteriorating public security situation on the main island of Guadalcanal and the Solomons need for assistance. Kemakeza's subsequent request for direct Australian aid in restoring law and order was within the long-established state practice regardless of any pressure that may have been exerted to elicit the legitimising request for external intervention.

Yet, it is clear that less publicly the Australian government felt that conditions in the Solomon Islands were slipping closer and closer to those of a failed state and that these changes could constitute a security risk to Australia itself. This view appears to have been heavily influenced by (as well as, perhaps, being reflected in) a think tank review of the Solomons and the implications for Australia.[9] The perspective of failed states as a contagion suggests intervention along the lines Prime Minister John Howard proposed in a *Sunday* television interview that one possibility was a pre-emptive strike to prevent internal collapse threatening other states.[10] His views on the value of direct, forceful intervention were undoubtedly bolstered in recent years by the successful interventions in East Timor and Bougainville. Embracing the concept of the failed state was a way of identifying possible sources of threat that might require direct military intervention.

Australia formally raised the failed states concept with regard to the Pacific Islands in September 2002 and in so doing joined the disparate group of Western states, led by the US, seeking to impose a renewed and more exacting commitment to state responsibility in pursuit of security. Foreign Minister Alexander Downer announced that the Commonwealth would link its aid in this region to issues of effective internal governance.[11] The minister's statement seemed clear enough at the time—roughly, it was a demand that regional states that were not 'performing' would have to do better to continue to receive Australian assistance. However, the Minister's statement contained a real carrot as well as the implied stick. Additional aid would be available to promote improved governance in the Pacific Islands region. Thus, the small scale of the states in this region appeared to alter the implications of the failed state concept as applied in the South Pacific; and began to move it more from the triage to the contagion models. The high-testosterone images of the intervention in the Solomon Islands appeared to complete this transition (especially in contrast with New Zealand's approach) and certainly contributed to Sir Michael Somare's reaction against Australia's wish to secure greater, and more direct, accountability from PNG for its aid.

So where to from here?

The attempts to adopt the concept of the failed state in the South Pacific have been rather desultory and opportunistic to date. The post-9/11 and post-Bali bombings paranoia in Australia has made a certain xenophobia respectable and border protection electorally popular. However, the dangers of failed states on the Commonwealth's doorstep do not appear to have been linked more than subjectively, and largely in passing, to the Bush administration's war on terrorism or to Canberra's part in this putative war. It seems doubtful that Australia (and even less likely that New Zealand) would take a lead in formalising the concept of the failed state as a means for circumscribing the doctrine of non-intervention in the internal affairs of a sovereign state in advance of a wider international movement. Rather than an intentional programme of rewriting international law, the concept of the failed state seems to be used on an *ad hoc* basis to stereotype and stigmatise. The term seems to be used mainly to suggest that the states in the South Pacific labelled as failed or failing should accept external intervention without protest since such intervention is 'necessary'. And, perhaps secondarily, having a failed state as a neighbour should silence critics in the intervening state since the dangers of this situation are deemed to be self-evidently unacceptable. Thus, while the concept itself may not be developed formally as grounds for intervention, the concerns raised abroad by the notion of failed states is resonating amongst states with South Pacific interests. Just how these concerns will be addressed is still emergent.

The small size and minor resource bases of most of the Pacific Island states makes them heavily dependent on external assistance, whether formal and direct as in the case of government-to-government aid or less formal and direct as in the case of remittances. Largely due to their limited capacities, the members of the regional community have developed some useful mitigation strategies over a fairly lengthy period. Chief amongst these has been the creation of a varied and robust regional system. Multilateral responses to some common problems have achieved certain economies of scale for member states of the various regional bodies. Perhaps more importantly, these organisations have greatly assisted their members in managing the diseconomies of scale that are an enduring feature of these states in meeting their responsibilities to their own citizens. Virtually all the Forum's members are archipelagoes and, therefore, governmental services must be provided across a number of islands without the benefit of any possible economies in the scale of their provision. In so far as the failure of a state to provide the necessary and expected services to its citizenry is a significant contributor to any criteria for identifying a failed state, this regional support mechanism for the Pacific Island states must constitute an important bulwark against state failure.

Because the regional system is an important factor in moderating the limitations of state incapacity, at least potentially, it is worth noting that an increased sensitivity to the concept of the failed state has not overtly drawn increased support for this system. This is especially true from the triage view of failed states since one might have expected a more concerted effort from Western states to support and strengthen this less intrusive mechanism for assisting PICs to meet their sovereign obligations. Building nation capacity has been an objective of the developmental programmes of virtually all the regional bodies and, for about a decade, pressure has been exerted through these bodies to improve standards of governance. This effort might be seen as an attempt to strengthen PIC member states by improving the operation of their administrative machinery.[12] But, if the triage model has not embraced the regional system enthusiastically, what of the relevance of regionalism to the contagion model?

Even the apparent use of the regional system to prop up a Solomon Islands in internal crisis is not what it appears from the contagion perspective on failed states. The intervention in the Solomon Islands in July 2003 began as a unilateral initiative and expanded to secure regional support later through the Pacific Islands Forum (largely based on the Biketawa Declaration[13]) to organise a regional response to instability in the Solomons.[14] Yet, the Forum's support for the intervention was not an altogether convincing fig leaf covering the Australian origins of the initiative. The Forum has had some difficulty over a long time in providing a mechanism for collective security in the region. The Fiji coups, New Caledonia, Bougainville and the Solomons prior to 2003 demonstrate the Pacific Islands Forum's reluctance at times in the past to perform an active security role.[15]

Perhaps, in the present climate of anxiety over failed states, the perception that unilateral intervention may be a consequence of external concerns over failed states will help to elevate collective security and a speedier delivery of remedial assistance to states under stress internally in regional system's priorities. If greater resources are made available to the region (whether multilaterally or bilaterally) the providers will insist on continuing improvements in PIC's governance procedures. In addition, the pressure on PICs with regard to the misuse of sovereign authority through poorly regulated offshore financial centres, the sale of passports, provision of flags of convenience and the like will increase. There can be little doubt that protecting their exercise of sovereignty will come at the price of greater compliance with international norms. It is a price that the PICs seem increasingly willing to pay as the chill in the global climate of international relations makes itself felt in the Pacific Islands.

Notes

1   The same may be said of the category failing states since this category is dependent on the notion of the failed state as an end point for a state increasingly incapable of meeting its sovereign responsibilities at home or abroad. This transition category is important for some theorists as a factor for proactive intervention but it will not be pursued in this chapter as the points to be made can be made using the failed state concept alone.

2   On the point of rogue states, I am aware that this term has had a peculiarly American usage in that country. There the term has generally implied four criteria to identify a rogue state. Such states are 1) overtly anti-American, 2) seek weapons of mass destruction, 3) abuse their own citizens and 4) offer support for terrorism. See: Meghan L. O'Sullivan, 'Sanctioning "Rogue" States: A Strategy in Decline?', *Harvard International Review*, (Summer 2000).

3   Jean Bodin is associated with the former interpretation through his *Six Books of the Commonwealth* (translated by M. J. Tooley (Oxford, Blackwell, 1955)) which was originally published in 1576. Thomas Hobbes provided one of the intellectual origins of modern power politics though his *Leviathan* (London, Dent, 1965) which was originally published in 1651.

4   R.H. Jackson, *Quasi-States: Sovereignty, International Relations and the Third World* (Cambridge, Cambridge University Press, 1990).

5   Gareth Evans and Mohamed Sahnoun, 'The Responsibility to Protect', *Foreign Affairs* 81, 6 (2002), pp.99–110.

6   Mary Locke and Jason Ladnier, 'Criteria for Military Intervention in Internal Wars: The Debate', *Regional Responses to Internal War*, The Fund for Peace, 2 (2001), p.1.

7   Robert H. Dorff refers to triage as the objective behind the concept of failed states in his

paper: 'State Failure and Responding to It', *Annual Convention of the International Studies Association* (New Orleans, 2002).

8   Gerald B. Helman and Steven R. Ratner, 'Saving Failed States', *Foreign Policy*, 89 (1992), pp.3–20.

9   Elsina Wainwright et al, *Our Failing Neighbour: Australia and the Future of Solomon Islands* (Canberra, The Australian Strategic Policy Institute, 2003). Although this report was published after the May meeting, the media reports at the time suggested that the government must have had advance knowledge of its content and recommendations.

10 WIN Television, *Sunday*, 1 December 2002.

11 'Australia shifts aid strategy for failed Pacific governments', *PacNews*, 26 September 2002.

12 A point that I would like to develop more fully later is that this post-Cold War emphasis on building state capacity may have missed the mark with regard to countries like the Solomon Islands. An assumption of a national unity where this has not yet been built has been a significant contributory factor in the recent instability. Freedom of movement and a right to purchase land regardless of customary practices made the state and its administrative organs a threat to those in Guadacanal unwilling to accept the rights of Malaitamen to 'their' land on the ground of being fellow Solomon Islanders. Building state capacity is not the same as nation building in a country as deeply fractured as the Solomons now appears to be.

13 Prompted by the Fijian and Solomon Islands crises, the Pacific Islands Forum meeting in 2000 adopted an Australian- and New Zealand-sponsored declaration at Biketawa in Kiribati that sought to provide for targeted measures to deal more authoritatively with political instability and to support democratic governance more strongly.

14 According to one well-placed source, the New Zealand government appears to have played a role in ensuring that Australia sought significant regional support for this initiative.

15 This is not to argue against the real value and effectiveness of the Pacific Islands regional institutions. I have spent most of my career arguing in favour of the value of these bodies in assisting the smaller PICs, particularly in providing support for meeting the obligations of sovereignty. However, not only have significant opportunities for achieving this objective not been taken, it has often not even been accepted that this role should be a direct objective of these organisations.

9

DIPLOMACY, POLITICS AND NUCLEAR TESTING: NEW ZEALAND CONFRONTS FRANCE 1995–96

Stephen Hoadley

Introduction

The issue of French nuclear testing arose as early as 1963 when the government of New Zealand delivered a formal note of protest on the occasion of France's first nuclear test in Algeria.[1] The issue sharpened when reports circulated in 1965 that France would move its testing to the South Pacific. France subsequently did so and, starting in 1966, conducted thirteen tests, each of which was protested by the New Zealand (NZ) government. Suspension of tests in 1968 eased NZ–French relations but resumption of tests in 1970 inflamed them once again, leading the Third Labour Government to dispatch a frigate to the test zone and initiate a case in the International Court of Justice (ICJ). France's unilateral decision to move tests underground brought the court case to a halt and eased relations, but continuation of tests in the 1980s, and the growth of the antinuclear movement and its support by the Fourth Labour Government, kept NZ–French relations unsettled.

In 1992, in response to the end of the Cold War, France suspended its test programme. In June 1995 France announced that a final test series would be conducted, however. This set in motion a series of events that comprise this case study.

Selective chronology of events

8 April 1992   France suspended South Pacific nuclear tests begun in 1966.
13 June 1995   The French president announced a resumption of nuclear testing in the South Pacific.

14 June 1995	New Zealand parliament debated the tests and the government imposed a military-contact freeze and subsequently took other measures.
6 August 1995	The first protest flotilla left Auckland.
12 August 1995	Prime Minister Jim Bolger dispatched HMNZS *Tui*.
5 September 1995	France began the test series.
7 September 1995	The New Zealand government requested the ICJ to reopen the 1974 injunction case; the ICJ rejected NZ's petition on 22 September 1995.
27 January 1996	France made its last test.
March 1996	France signed the South Pacific Nuclear Free Zone (SPNFZ) protocols and the Comprehensive Test Ban Treaty (CTBT).
23 September 1996	Foreign Minister Don McKinnon wrote to his French counterpart to say, 'I am very pleased that relations between our two countries are now back on a sound footing.'

Demands by opposition MPs

The French announcement in June 1995 also triggered an emotional political debate in the House of Representatives as to how New Zealand should respond. The opposition MPs were particularly radical in their proposals. A summary of their demands is presented below:
- protest directly to President Chirac and urge other leaders, particularly Britain's John Major, to join the protest
- send delegations to the United Nations (UN) and other international fora to rally protests
- suspend France's dialogue partner status in the South Pacific Forum
- reopen the 1974 ICJ case against nuclear testing and support the current challenge of the legality of nuclear weapons
- dispatch a navy frigate to the test site as was done in 1973
- sponsor a protest boat crewed by indigenous persons to show solidarity with Kanaks and Polynesians
- send the French ambassador home and recall New Zealand's ambassador from Paris
- refuse to recognise French diplomatic passports

- refuse the customary official apology when New Zealand protesters burn the French flag
- boycott French goods and discourage French tourists
- demand access to the test site for placement of monitoring equipment by New Zealand or International Atomic Energy Agency scientists
- challenge the legality of the twelve-mile exclusion zone around the test site
- encourage New Zealanders to flood French government offices and news media with fax and phone protest messages
- support industrial action to disrupt communications with French diplomatic posts and impede French shipping and aircraft movements in the South Pacific
- back indigenous movements to declare independence and expel France from the South Pacific.

The government response

The government, responsible for wider relations with France in the longer term and aware of New Zealand's vulnerability to French trade sanctions, was more cautious. Nevertheless the government did cancel or postpone seven events on the calendar of NZ–French relations. These included:

1. a Royal New Zealand Air Force Command and Staff College staff course visit to New Caledonia
2. port calls to Noumea by HMNZS *Waikato, Endeavour,* and *Wellington*
3. an army platoon exchange with French units based in New Caledonia
4. visits to New Zealand ports by French naval vessels
5. training or routine transportation flights to New Zealand by French military aircraft
6. negotiations on acquisition of all French military equipment, including a helicopter and a French man-portable air defence missile system
7. government sponsorship of a visit by veterans to New Caledonia for VJ Day commemorations.

Prudence prevails

Prudence was urged by officials from the Ministry of Foreign Affairs and Trade (MFAT), and their advice appears to have had a moderating effect. While the seven events above were curtailed, they were isolated in the wider context of the relationship with France. The following six links were maintained, namely:

1. all flights related to aeromedical, evacuation, search and rescue, maritime surveillance, and Antarctic support
2. VIP flights on a case-by-case basis
3. exchanges between children of defence personnel of both countries
4. meetings of the French–New Zealand Friendship Fund
5. attendance at World War II, World War I, and national day ceremonies (with the level of representation to be reviewed)
6. diplomatic contacts (with their level to be reviewed).

Public opinion and protest

These diplomatic distinctions were not appreciated by the wider public. Public opinion, informed and in some cases encouraged by the media, was captivated by the issue and turned sharply in favour of stronger action by the government. A majority approved various stronger alternatives ranging from boycott to a diplomatic freeze to an international complaint; curtailment of an All Black tour was however rejected, which may illustrate something about New Zealand's popular culture.

NZ Public Opinion on Government Action Against France Percentage (rounded) in July 1995 supporting selected options

NZ government should complain to the United Nations	91 %
NZ government should take direct action	86 %
NZ government should protest more strongly	81 %
NZ government should send a frigate to Mururoa	63 %
NZ government should close France's posts in NZ	63 %
NZ government should cut all ties with France	62 %
NZ government should close its posts in France	55 %
NZ government should refuse to buy French products 'favoured'	>50 %
NZ government should cancel All Black tour of France	39 %

Source: Research International New Zealand media statement 'Huge support for direct action against France', 11 July 1995 and author's estimate.

With the support of public opinion, and widely reported by the press, New Zealanders engaged in the following forms of protest:
- demonstrations, speeches, media articles by non-government organisations (NGOs) and churches
- consumer boycott called by the Council of Trade Unions
- The Warehouse and Noel Leeming announced no buying of goods from France
- Novotel canceled a Bastille Day booking by the Alliance Française
- Akaroa considered cancelling the annual commemoration of its founding by French settlers
- Dr John Hinchcliff, head of Auckland Institute (later University) of Technology, organised a delegation of fifty mayors, councillors and educators to take the protest to France
- a delegation including MPs and mayors flew to Papeete to join independence protests there
- a protest flotilla of private boats, including one planned to have Australian legislators aboard (which never showed up) formed up to sail to Mururoa to protest.

Subsequent government actions

The government appears to have been moved by the spontaneous upsurge of criticism of France and advocacy of stronger New Zealand protest actions. The government then supplemented its initial seven actions by ten further actions. These included the following:
1. Prime Minister Jim Bolger wrote to ninety heads of state as follows: 'I would ask you to consider raising with President Chirac and his government the concerns we have over the planned resumption of nuclear testing in the South Pacific.'
2. cabinet supported discussion in the South Pacific Forum Regional Action Committee (but as an exercise in regional public information, not a diplomatic campaign against France)
3. the government drafted a UN General Assembly resolution seeking an immediate end to French nuclear testing
4. diplomats persuaded the Association of South East Asian Nations Regional Forum meeting in Brunei to issue a call for an end to nuclear tests

5   New Zealand delegates sponsored a resolution at the October 1995 Conference of the Inter-Parliamentary Union
6   New Zealand delegates attached a protest statement to the communiqué of the Commonwealth Heads of Government meeting, despite the vigorous opposition by Britain's John Major
7   the government persisted with an antinuclear submission already planned for the ICJ advisory opinion
8   cabinet decided to attempt to reopen New Zealand's 1974 ICJ injunction case
9   the Minister of Foreign Affairs recalled the New Zealand ambassador from Paris ('as a mark of New Zealand's outrage,' the prime minister announces)
10 the government dispatched HMNZS *Tui* to the test site, but only as a 'silent witness' not to enter the French exclusion zone or assist the private protest vessels save in emergencies.

New Zealand proposals for diplomatic damage control in 1996

France was experiencing criticism not just from New Zealand but from many quarters, domestically as well as internationally. Its leaders appear to have been moved to respond to restore a degree of harmony. France announced a reduction of the number of tests and in January 1996 announced the completion of the test series. MFAT saw this as an opening for New Zealand to explore ways to restore the relationship to its previous cordiality. Officials prepared a list of proposals, as follows:

- an invitation to the director general of the French Foreign Ministry to visit New Zealand, returning a visit by Richard Nottage prior to the onset of testing (but a ministerial visit, and a visit by a French National Assembly delegation, were ruled out as 'premature')
- welcome to a visit by an AXA/CNPF (Consiel National du Patron Français) insurance industry delegation
- encouragement of rugby and yachting contacts
- trilateral talks to coordinate New Zealand, Australian, and French aid in the South Pacific
- establishment of a Taupo–Noumea sister-city relationship
- increase in New Zealand scholarships to students from New Caledonia.

'Conditional' steps to re-establishing full military links

The government was determined not to return diplomatic relations to 'normal' unless France made further moves to demonstrate sincerity. Ministers were frank in citing hostile New Zealand public opinion as a reason for not hurrying the restoration of relations. Diplomatic correspondence ensued, in which New Zealand set conditions and France replied with surprise, pointing out that it was New Zealand that curtailed relations, so it was up to New Zealand to restore them. MFAT officials continued to devise damage control proposals, and in the course of 1996 the government took the following steps to foster military relations, the sector most severely affected:

- French patrol boat (but not navy ship) accompanied the Auckland–Noumea yacht race fleet
- the same French patrol boat berthed at HMNZS *Philomel* jetty (but not to exercise with any Royal New Zealand Navy ship)
- a visit was planned by a French warship (but no exercise)
- a visit was planned by French military aircraft (but no exercise)
- an RNZAF Orion landed at Tontouta airfield in New Caledonia
- a visit was made by the commander of French forces in the Pacific
- exchange visits were made by New Zealand Defence Force and French officers
- negotiations on buying the Mistral missile system were resumed
- France was included in TASMANEX naval exercises
- limited non-combat military unit cooperation occured during a disaster relief mission to the South Pacific
- trilateral (with Australia) maritime surveillance coordination was reinvigorated.

In the course of 1996 France signed the protocols of the Treaty of Rarotonga, and the CTBT, and closed its Pacific test centre. New Zealand reciprocated with a warm statement restoring at least rhetorical harmony in September 1996. A residue of suspicion, resulting not only from this test series but also from prior tests, and the *Rainbow Warrior* bombing, may have persisted in many New Zealanders' minds, but at the official level relations resumed a 'normal' course. In subsequent years NZ–French cooperation in the South Pacific has steadily deepened. MFAT's 'damage control' during the trying period of 1995–96 appears to have been successful in preventing irreparable damage to the longer-term relationship.

Political Summary

To summarise the politics of the case study, I have composed the following diagram, in which players are arrayed on a spectrum from strong through moderate anti-French-testing views, to ambivalence and indifference, and at the other end of the spectrum where there is support for either testing or France or both.

Spectrum of Opinion on French Nuclear Tests 1995–96

Strong antitesting	Moderate antitesting	Balancing multiple interests, cautious, neutral	Pro-testing, indifferent, or pro- France
NZ opposition MPs	NZ Cabinet, especially Bolger and McKinnon	NZ Ministry of Foreign Affairs and Trade	President of France
NZ antinuclear movement, especially Greenpeace, CND*, PMA*, peace NGOs	Australia	ACT party	Ministry of Foreign Affairs of France
Churches	Micronesian governments	Polynesian governments especially Cook Islands	European governments
Protest skippers	ASEAN governments	US Government	Some Francophone non-aligned movement governments
Warehouse, Watties, Noel Leeming	US Congress	ICJ	
Council of Trade Unions	UN General Assembly Fourth Committee	Various international orgnisations	
NZ public opinion			
Melanesian governments			
Non-Aligned Movement governments			
French and European antinuclear			

Conclusion

It is tempting to see this episode as an example of successful protest by New Zealand in curtailing French testing and inducing signature by France of nuclear arms control agreements. The case also reveals some evidence of the success of opposition MPs, the antinuclear movement and the general public in pushing the New Zealand government to take stronger actions than it initially intended or than the officials of MFAT recommended. In my view the latter is more plausible than the former, not least because many other players were mobilised against French testing, as the diagram shows, so New Zealand's role should not be exaggerated.

But beyond the question of who influenced whom, the case clearly illustrates the differing views that arise in New Zealand in response to a provocative event abroad, and the differing actions by the government and the public that can be taken, or avoided, in response. It illustrates, thereby, the interaction of domestic politics with New Zealand's foreign policy, and it provides a glimpse of how MFAT officials arrive at their recommendations to government, and why government ministers adopt, or ignore, these recommendations.

Note

1   This chapter is drawn from a monograph entitled 'New Zealand and France: Diplomacy Disputes and Negotiations' to be published in 2005, in which full documentation of sources may be found.

10

SOUTH-WEST PACIFIC: ARC OF INSTABILITY OR MATRIX OF DISCONTENT?[1]

Jon Fraenkel

The presence of an 'arc of instability' in the South-West Pacific has attracted increasing concern ever since the coups in Fiji and Solomon Islands in May and June 2000.[2] Curving eastwards from Aceh (Indonesia) through Mindanao (Philippines), East Timor, West Papua, Papua New Guinea (PNG) and Bougainville, and then downwards through Solomon Islands to Fiji in the east, this arc has been described as 'the human and political equivalent of the tectonic fault line that stretches around the Pacific Rim'.[3] In the 'eye of the storm', so this disturbing topography suggests, sits northern Australia, surrounded by failing or conflict-ridden states.[4] What is less often appreciated is that the expression 'arc of instability' is not unique to the Pacific. 'Arcs of instability' are currently identified in the Balkans, in Uzbekistan, Tajikistan and Chechnya, in West Africa, in the Middle East, and in North Korea, South-East Asia, the Caribbean, the Indian Ocean, and even Columbia and the Andean region.[5] Authorship has been attributed, not only to Australian National University professors,[6] but also to American military planners, European think tanks, and even Russia's President.[7]

The initial geopolitical reference-point was the Middle East.[8] Speaking at a North Atlantic Treaty Organisation (NATO) conference in Barcelona on 26 May 1998, General Klaus Naumann warned of an 'arc of instability' on Europe's periphery, running 'from the Maghreb to the Indian Ocean'.[9]

'Arcs of crisis' had earlier been identified in Africa, North-East Asia and the northwest of South America.[10] 'Arc of instability', it seems plausible, is a milder version of 'arc of crisis'. The two terms are often used interchangeably, but the former provides the softer option. An adjacent 'arc' seems preferable to being encircled or semicircled by troublesome states, and 'instability' is less threatening than 'crisis'. Both terms convey the impression of a serious, yet manageable, security threat. If so, the ultimate originator was United States (US) president Jimmy Carter's national security adviser, Zbigniew

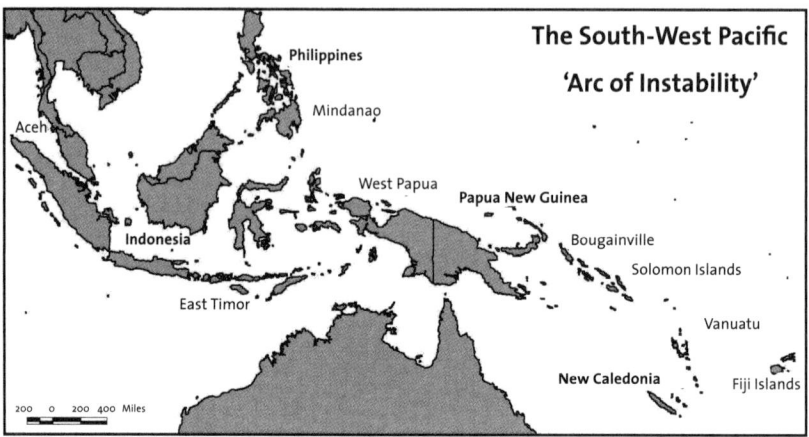

Brzezinski, who in 1978 described the southern tier of states reaching beneath the Soviet Union from Egypt to Pakistan as an 'arc of crisis'.[11] The term was subsequently used for historical purposes to describe the Middle East as a whole during 1973–87 in the *Encyclopaedia Brittanica*.[12]

Perhaps this breadth of application and these origins of the phrase 'arc of instability' may serve to highlight potential problems associated with the recycling of second-hand concepts to investigate Pacific crises. Media coverage of regional conflicts has regularly borrowed descriptions from elsewhere, as with the use of the terms 'Balkanisation' or 'ethnic cleansing' to describe the troubles in Fiji and the Solomon Islands.[13] Sometimes these borrowed analogies can be useful and informative, or at least can inform fruitful contrasts or comparisons. At other times, particularly when driven by incautious headline-hungry editors, they can be deeply misleading.

Unfortunately, the overnight media response, understandably driven by tight deadlines and insufficient time for research of what are admittedly complex situations, frequently drives the more analytical debate. For example, after the coup in the Solomon Islands (5 June 2000) quickly followed that in Fiji (19 May 2000), many commentators concluded the next day that a 'copycat' or 'demonstration effect' was at work. This verdict did not arise from intelligence reports of clandestine connections, but was simply a ready-to-hand way of explaining the seemingly unintelligible crisis in the Solomon Islands as if this were merely a repeat of the more familiar events so recently witnessed in neighbouring Fiji. Similarly, the rather knee-jerk, journalistic depiction of the Pacific as experiencing 'tribal' or 'African'-style difficulties was subsequently echoed in the scholarly literature.[14]

That said, I see little reason to object to the phrase arc of instability. Who can deny that the Solomon Islands, Fiji, Bougainville, West Papua, Aceh and East Timor are, or have been, unstable? All have recently either witnessed coups, secessionist crises or varying degrees of civil warfare. And whether or not conflicts occur in a curvaceous shape seems a rather sterile line of inquiry. So I am willing to use the phrase, with the rider that given its extraordinary generality of application, it seems doubtful whether much that is of value can be squeezed from this. Shorn of its contours, all that is left is the reference to 'instability'. So surely the more pressing issues concern the nature and causes of that instability and what can or should be done about this. This chapter focuses on the Melanesian end of that arc, stretching from West Papua eastwards, although it also draws some contrasts, more broadly, with other parts of the Oceania region.

Often, discussion of the Melanesian arc of instability, and the associated emphasis on state failure, goes hand-in-hand with a call for greater antipodean intervention of some kind. Two influential think tanks, the Australian Strategic Policy Institute and the Centre for Independent Studies, called in mid-2003 for a major paradigm shift in Australia's Pacific policy. Both emphasised the presence of a Pacific arc of instability, and both recycled perceived threats from other parts of the globe. The Centre for Independent Policy Studies argued in favour of abandoning the long-standing 'hands-off' approach of respecting PNG's sovereign right to make its own choices',[15] and highlighted 'open warlordism in Bougainville, Solomon Islands and the New Guinea Highlands'. 'The prospect not merely of a failed state, but a rogue state (like those of Amin, Mobutu, Bokassa and Mugabe in Africa),' it claimed, 'cannot be lightly dismissed.'[16] The more influential government-financed Australian Strategic Policy Institute (ASPI) pamphlet *Our Failing Neighbour: Australia and the Future of the Solomon Islands* depicted the Solomon Islands as a 'post-modern badlands' and a 'Petri dish in which transnational and non-state security threats can develop and flourish'. Among these threats, 'international criminal organisations', 'drug-smuggling', 'identity fraud', 'people smuggling' and 'perhaps even terrorism' were identified.[17]

Plausibly, the Petri dish scenarios were just rhetorical flourishes designed to galvanise otherwise reluctant metropolitan politicians into action (or an unconcerned public to accept action) by taking advantage of the post-Bali bombing and post-Iraq War readiness to engage overseas in the 'War against Terrorism'. If so, they received the desired response. Australian prime minister John Howard told the Sydney Institute on 1 July 2003 that 'we know that a failed state in our region, on our doorstep, will jeopardise our own security'. 'Rogue and failed states,' he argued, 'become a base from which terrorists and transnational criminals organise their operations, train their recruits and manage their finances . . . the best thing we can do is to take remedial action and take it now.'[18] Foreign Minister Alexander Downer, more cautiously, acknowledged that 'we don't have evidence that the South Pacific has been a haven for terrorism. What I would say is that a failed state is a state that *could possibly* be exploited by terrorists.'[19]

As in the pre-Iraq War discussions, a mixture of different reasons were given for the 2000-strong Australian-led intervention force that arrived in the Solomon Islands in late July. 'Smoking guns', apparently, were not required, but the goal was nonetheless pre-emptive intervention and was explicitly advanced as a major shift in region-wide, rather than Solomons-specific policy. Australia's participation in the US-led intervention in Iraq provided the diplomatic impetus to the paradigm shift in South Pacific regional policy. Alternatively, this was depicted as inspired by a new doctrine of 'cooperative intervention', predicated upon a clear 'act of consent' by the Solomon Islands government, and aimed at tackling what were primarily internal security threats.[20] Many Solomon Islanders understandably backed Australian intervention to deal with former militia leaders who refused to disarm in the wake of the Townsville Peace Agreement of October 2000, and continued to terrorise the population and bankrupt the state. Operation 'Helpem Fren' (pidgin for 'help a friend'), endorsed by an act of consent passed through the Solomon Islands parliament, was carefully crafted to avoid allegations of neo-colonialism.[21] Yet the willingness to go beyond disarming the militants and playing a security role to taking over key positions within the civil service suggests a longer-run engagement.

Among Pacific analysts it is broadly agreed that the major security threats in the Pacific Island region remain internal rather than external.[22] Although borders are often poorly policed and passport scams, notably in the Marshall Islands, PNG and the Solomon Islands, open avenues for identity fraud, the small closely knit and often predominantly rural societies of Oceania would prove an inhospitable target for terrorist cells. Muslim cleric Abdul Majid, who was alleged to have been at university with al-Qaeda's Osama bin Laden, was expelled from Fiji in February 2003, after eighteen years residence.[23] But there is no evidence that Fiji's dispersed Muslim population provides any easy target for Islamic fundamentalist militants. Tongan and Marshallese-registered ships have been identified as 'flags of convenience' for terrorist outfits and offshore banking facilities have been held to provide money laundering opportunities.[24] Yet most of these stories, including most absurdly reported al-Qaeda links with the southern highlands of PNG,[25] have proved false. Weak states, like those in the Solomon Islands, and perhaps PNG and Nauru, show few signs of attaining the level of coherence required by genuinely rogue states.

Instability in the Solomon Islands was connected with the state's loss of its monopoly over the use of armed force and even loss of control over its own territory outside the capital, Honiara. Few of the non-indigenes who form the majority in the Honiara Town Council area felt able to set foot beyond Henderson Airport in the east or Kakabona to the west. In the extreme west of the Solomons group, only a few miles separate the Shortland Islands and Choiseul from Bougainville (PNG). During and after the 2000 coup crisis, Bougainville Revolutionary Army (BRA) militants proved able to cross international borders undeterred, on high-powered speedboats. At the invitation of the Provincial Council, the BRA even played a policing role in the Western Province, rather indiscriminately resisting feared encroachments by the Malaita Eagle Forces. During the following months, six of the Solomons' nine provinces threatened to break away, or seek looser national-level arrangements.[26] The Townsville Peace Agreement (TPA) required the government to establish a 'Constitutional Council to rewrite the Constitution' to provide for 'more autonomy by devolution or by constitutional amendment to effect self-governing status'.[27] The consequent constitutional review, still underway, may result in the nation being organised along looser federal lines. In these senses, the Solomon Islands state has become a state in name only.

When the conflict in the Solomon Islands commenced in late 1998, people from the island of Malaita formed the bulk of the population of the capital Honiara on the island of Guadalcanal and a sizeable fraction of the rural population on Guadalcanal's fertile northern plains. In late 1998 and 1999 the Guadalcanal Revolutionary Army (GRA, or later Isatabu Freedom Movement—henceforth, IFM) chased 24,000 or so Malaitan settlers from their homes on rural Guadalcanal. Many crowded into the capital and formed their own rival militia group, the Malaita Eagle Forces (MEF). The MEF raided the police armoury at Auki (on Malaita) in January 2000 and seized additional weaponry from the Alligator Creek police checkpoint on

16 May 2000 (notably, three days *before* the supposedly copied Fiji coup). There was clear evidence of police complicity in both raids. The Police Field Force subsequently participated in a 'joint operation' with the MEF to overthrow the elected government on 5 June 2000, removing reformist premier, Bartholomew Ulufa'alu. Ulufa'alu had earlier appealed in vain for armed Australian and New Zealand assistance, having seen the possibility of an MEF takeover in April.[28]

The coup leaders steered clear of abrogating the 1978 constitution, and sought to preserve a semblance of legality during the transition process. The High Court found that this had occurred under duress, but upheld the Governor General's decision to endorse the parliamentary selection of a new prime minister, Mannaseh Sogavare.[29] Instead of transforming the state into a vehicle for ethnic supremacy or carrying out threats of all-out war against the IFM, MEF militants, police officers and a number of leading politicians repeatedly sought to extort as much financial compensation as possible from it, generously assisted by sizeable cash grants from the Republic of Taiwan and by advances from the Central Bank. State compensation, dressed up as authentic Melanesian custom, was a crucial demand of both Malaitan and Guadalcanalese provincial leaders.

The peace settlement agreed in October 2000 at Townsville (Queensland, Australia) brought an end to the fighting and fresh elections were held in December 2001, but over 500 high-powered weapons remained at large.[30] The result was not a postmodern Petri dish for breeding supranational security threats, but the internal security situation was nevertheless serious. Between 2000 and 2003, the judicial and prison systems were scarcely operational. For example, former police commissioner, Sir Fred Soaki, was murdered point-blank by a police officer in February 2003. The murderer was captured, and imprisoned, but proved able to escape, probably with the connivance of *wantoks*[31] within the security forces. Extortion of state revenue by militant leaders left little cash for government services. Civil servants went for weeks without pay, and education and health services were run down, particularly in rural areas. Gross domestic product (GDP) per capita fell by over a third during 2000–02.[32]

Further towards the east, in Fiji, the state possesses far greater coherence, but here too the prospects for a durable 'rogue state' seem remote. A coup back in 1987 put into office a government that reserved the premiership and presidency for ethnic Fijians, and stacked the parliamentary seat distribution against the Indo-Fijians. Yet even that regime never looked like becoming a rogue state. By the mid-1990s, coup leader Sitiveni Rabuka reversed those discriminatory provisions, and put in place a new constitution designed to establish a multiethnic government bringing together the political leaders of the country's two major ethnic groups.

At the first elections under the new system, in 1999, that constitution did not work as expected. Voters instead turned away from those parties that had brokered the constitutional compromise, and instead the Fiji Labour Party emerged with an absolute majority.[33] Mahendra Chaudhry became the country's first ever Indo-Fijian prime minister, at the head of a coalition government that included several smaller, largely ethnic Fijian-backed parties. On his government's first anniversary, it was overthrown in a coup mounted by indigenous Fijian extremists led by George Speight. Yet, here again, a potential 'rogue' regime proved unsustainable. The security forces laid siege around parliament, while Speight and the would-be coup perpetrators held the former government hostage inside for fifty-six days.[34] The military did, however, remove the former president Ratu Sir Kamisese Mara from office, and issued a decree purporting to abrogate the 1997 constitution. When the law courts upheld that constitution in a landmark judgement in March 2001, the postcoup interim government that had been installed by the military accepted the verdict and called fresh elections.[35] Held in August 2001 these were described as 'free and fair' by both Commonwealth and UN observers.[36] Constitutional uncertainties nonetheless remain, owing to the new government's reluctance to stand by the multiparty cabinet provisions in the 1997 constitution.[37]

Still further eastwards, the arc of instability gives way to a region of extraordinary stability. In Tonga, the king and nobility select twenty-one of the thirty parliamentarians. Only nine are popularly elected. The nobility benefits from a systematic 'redistribution from poor to rich'. 'The puzzle is why the public let them get away with it,' concluded departing New Zealand high commissioner Brian Smythe in a letter leaked in June 2003. 'At a time of unrest in Melanesia,' he continued, 'the stability in Tonga has had a certain appeal—but it is stability that covers over deep cracks which call for remedial measures.'[38] Tonga has problems associated with youth unemployment, a weak educational system and slow economic growth, but per capita GDP is twice that of the Solomon Islands. As with neighbouring Samoa, Niue and the Cook Islands, over 50 per cent of Tongans live overseas, mainly in the United States, Australia or New Zealand, and prop up the country's balance of payments by large remittance flows. Overseas migration provides a crucial safety valve, enabling younger Tongans to escape the rigidities of the domestic hierarchical system. This also provides a supranational dimension to the country's politics and support for the domestic prodemocracy movement. In February 2003, King Taufa'ahau Tupou IV banned the entry of the New Zealand-published independent newspaper, *Taimi 'o Tonga* (*Times of Tonga*), until the Supreme Court ruled his actions illegal. The monarch-controlled government responded by passing legislation restricting freedom of the press.

Most Pacific Island countries are amongst the world's least 'rogue'-like states. Many are dependent territories or freely associated with metropolitan powers. In the northern Pacific, the Republic of the Marshall Islands, Federated States of Micronesia, and Palau all have 'Compacts of Free Association' with the United States, and all figured amongst the 'Coalition of the Willing' during the Iraq War.[39] Guam, the Commonwealth of the Northern Marianas, and American Samoa are still more tightly integrated with the USA. France retains control over New Caledonia, Wallis and Futuna, and French Polynesia, while Niue and the Cook Islands are freely associated with New Zealand. The Pacific has the highest levels of aid per capita in the world. Where export industries exist, they are mostly reliant on preferential trade agreements with the metropolitan countries. High levels of import consumption prevail, mostly sourced from metropolitan powers around the Pacific Rim. Pacific Islander elites regularly travel overseas and, even in the case of the Tongan aristocracy, are deeply influenced by Western values and traditions (a factor that notably contributes to the disdain they have for their own peoples).[40]

The Polynesian and Micronesian countries are, for the most part, ethnically and linguistically homogeneous,[41] whereas Melanesia is home to perhaps a quarter of the world's total language stock. What influence, if any, does this have on the contrasting propensity for political conflict? In PNG, West Papua, Vanuatu and the Solomon Islands ethno-linguistic diversity, on the one hand, contributes to difficulties in postcolonial state-building, but, on the other hand, diminishes the capacity of elites to use direct ethnic appeals as a means of securing political power. Leaving aside the Polynesian outliers, accumulation-oriented Melanesian 'big man' systems provide a less durable and resilient foundation for postcolonial state-formation than the hierarchical chiefly systems to the east.[42] The regularity of 'no confidence' votes and regime turnover in the Solomon Islands and PNG, and the extraordinary brevity of average MP incumbency, are symptomatic of this more fluid Melanesian leadership style.[43]

Fiji is exceptional, not just in the Pacific, but also internationally (along with Guyana), in having a long-standing bipolar division between two relatively homogeneous ethnic groups. Indigenous Fijians make up around 52 per cent of the population, Indo-Fijians around 44 per cent, and the 'others', mainly Chinese, part-Europeans and 'other Pacific Islanders', account for only around 5 per cent of the population. Intra-ethnic cleavages exist, for example, between Indo-Fijians descended from those who embarked from the north and south of the Indian subcontinent or Hindus

Table 1. Human development and ethnolinguistic diversity indicators for the Pacific Islands countries, 1998

	Real GDP per capita (US$) (1)	Life expectancy at birth (2)	Adult literacy rate % (3)	Ethno-linguistic diversity* (4)
Polynesia				
Cook Islands	4,947	72.0	93.2	5
Niue	3,714	74.0	97.0	2
Tonga	1,868	68.0	99.0	3
Samoa	1,060	66.6	95.7	2
Tuvalu	1,157	67.0	95.0	2
Micronesia				
Palau	8,027	69.0	91.4	4
Nauru	3,450	58.2	95.0	3
Micronesia, Fed. States	2,070	65.7	71.3	17
Marshall Islands	1,182	65.0	74.4	2
Kiribati	702	61.6	92.2	2
Melanesia				
Fiji Islands	2,684	66.5	92.9	10
Vanuatu	1,231	65.8	33.5	109
Solomon Islands	926	64.7	30.3	69
Papua New Guinea	1,196	54.0	28.2	832

Source: United Nations Develpoment Programme, *Pacific Human Development Report 1999*, Suva, 1999; Summer Institute of Linguistics, Ethnologue.com.

* Ethno-linguistic is measured using the Summer Institute of Linguistics estimates of numbers of 'living languages', unadjusted to exclude common languages such as pidgin, or imported languages such as English and French.

and Muslims, but predictions that these would be manifested in intra-ethnic fissions at the polls have proved repeatedly false. Likewise, the indigenous Fijian confederacies (Tovata, Kubuna and Burebasaga) provide potential sources of intra-Fijian frictions, as do the much overplayed divisions between the west and east of Viti Levu or between the heavily Tongan-influenced Lau Islanders and those on mainland Viti Levu.

Yet recent political history does not vindicate the regularly heard claims that intra-Fijian frictions were somehow 'more important' than Fijian/Indo-Fijian cleavages. After the 2001 polls, a single political party (*Soqosoqo ni Duavata ni Lewenivanua*—SDL), which had endorsement both from key Fijian power brokers on mainland Viti Levu (Naitasiri, Rewa) and the Lau Provincial Council, proved able to take nearly all the majority Fijian seats on mainland Viti Levu and Lau. Contrary to predictions that the western Viti Levu-based (and chronically misnamed) Party of National Unity, which was closely allied with Labour, would perform well, it lost all its seats to the SDL. The major new fission at the 2001 polls, was between the SDL and the newly formed Matanitu Vanua, a party that temporarily counted imprisoned would-be coup leader George Speight amongst its MPs.

Fiji, following Arthur Lewis's expression, is 'integrated by day, but separated by night'. Intermarriage is rare, and ethnic divisions follow similar lines to religious differences (between predominantly Hindu and Muslim Indo-Fijians, and largely Christian ethnic Fijians). Ethnic identification strongly influences political loyalties. At the last elections in 2001, the major Fijian parties were able to obtain less than 1 per cent of the Indo-Fijian vote, while the largely Indo-Fijian-backed parties secured less than 3 per cent of the ethnic Fijian vote. The country's politics have obstinately revolved around bipolar tensions between ethnic Fijians and Indo-Fijians. Election victories by parties largely reliant on the Indo-Fijian vote have in each case led to constitutional crises (1977) or coups (1987 and 2000).

Despite that bipolarity, Fiji has not witnessed high levels of communal violence. Not a single death occurred during the 1987 coup. In the wake of the 19 May 2000 takeover of parliament, a succession of clashes between rebels and the security forces resulted in a total of sixteen deaths,[44] but none resulted from direct ethnically based clashes between ethnic Fijians and Indo-Fijians. There were, however, attacks on Indo-Fijian property, particularly in the vicinity of George Speight's home village in northern Tailevu and in parts of northern Vanua Levu. Frictions in Fiji are primarily focused at the political level, not as an indigenous challenge to Indo-Fijian citizenship or commercial rights,[45] but rather centred on political rights and control over the state apparatus.

Recent multicountry investigations of the likelihood of civil war have suggested little correlation between ethnic heterogeneity and instability. 'Ethnic and religious diversity does not make a society more dangerous,' argues Collier, 'in fact, it makes it safer.'[46] Similarly, Fry argues that 'ethnonationalist crises' are unlikely either in the more homogeneous Polynesian states or the more diverse Melanesian states, but become more likely in ethnically bipolar states like Fiji. 'Until recently,' he explains, '[Fiji] appeared to be the only postcolonial society in the Pacific that had this ethnic structure . . . But recently it has been joined by the Solomon Islands [which] . . . has effectively become more like Fiji in ethnic structure.'[47]

Yet it is not solely bipolar ethnic structures that drive political conflict in Melanesia. The Solomon Islands situation was very different to that in Fiji. The combined Guadalcanalese/Malaitan share of the population, including those in the Honiara Town Council area, is 56.7 per cent,[48] whereas in Fiji, Indo-Fijians and ethnic Fijians make up 95 per cent of the population. Religious affiliations are mixed on both Guadalcanal and Malaita, and, unlike Fiji, intermarriage is frequent. Solomon Islands governments have always, inevitably, had mixed representation from different parts of the group.

Insofar as the Solomon Islands 'became more like Fiji', the question is why. Both Malaita and Guadalcanal had numerous distinct ethnic groups, if, following Esman, by 'ethnic group' one means groups that share a common language, distinctive customs or perception of a common destiny.[49] Both militias (the IFM and MEF) were, in this sense, supra-ethnic organisations, although the camps established by the MEF around Honiara during mid-2000 were manned by the different north Malaitan ethnic groups (Kwaio, Lau, To'ambaita, Kwara'ae, etc). Significant tensions existed within both the MEF and IFM, and after the Townsville Agreement these generated considerable infighting. The 1998–99 island-wide identities had not sprung up overnight. In both cases, there were precedents. The Maasina Ruru movement had emerged on Malaita during 1944–52 and spread to other islands, until forcibly suppressed by the British colonial authorities. On Guadalcanal, the Weather Coast-based Moro movement emerged in the late 1950s and gathered significant support across the island.[50] The term 'Isatabu', adopted by the IFM militias in place of the Spanish-bequeathed word 'Guadalcanal', was inherited from the Moro movement. Ethnic fragmentation did not, in itself, preclude the emergence of island-wide insurgent movements.

Second, two other overseas-controlled Pacific territories have witnessed violent internecine conflict despite a high degree of ethnic heterogeneity. In West Papua, which has perhaps 263 distinct ethno-linguistic groups as well as a large Indonesian immigrant population, a low intensity civil war aimed at securing independence or autonomy has been waged by the *Organisasi Papua Merdeka* (Movement for Free Papua) since the 1960s. In New Caledonia, politicians representing the 44 per cent indigenous Kanaks lent their support to a militant independence movement in the 1980s. With a partial settlement of that conflict, clashes have become frequent between Kanaks and the minority Wallisian population, particularly in areas around the capital, Noumea.[51]

Third, confining attention to postcolonial Pacific states, PNG may have 832 distinct living languages, but it has nevertheless witnessed protracted conflict between the BRA and PNG Defence Force in the period 1989–98, although there was also fighting amongst Bougainvilleans themselves. Tension or violent conflict in fact frequently assumes a regional or quasi-'ethnic' form, even where groups may be highly heterogeneous.[52] Clashes in the squatter settlements around Port Moresby have pitted 'Papuans' against 'highlanders'. As Trompf found:

> In urban centres . . . tit-for-tat manslaying is capable of being played out on a regional rather than purely local basis . . . people who speak the same language, even if hailing from traditionally hostile tribes in the countryside, tend to cooperate and support one another in towns. The *wantok* principle can operate towards . . . town dwellers gravitating into wider cultural or *regional* groupings which bear enmity towards each other and thus place payback on a newer, though more thinly spread footing.[53]

Vanuatu, which again is highly linguistically diverse, also experienced post independence quasi-bipolar conflict focused, oddly, around the division between 'francophone' and 'Anglophone' factions.

Although ethnic heterogeneity may diminish the prospects for violent conflict it does not preclude this. In postcolonial Melanesia, low per capita GDP, high population growth rates, and rapid urbanisation have ensured that the growth of formal employment is too small to soak up the annual flow of school leavers.[54] In the Solomon Islands, the 'Masta Liu' phenomenon became a local cultural symbol, referring to the urbanised underemployed youth, often disenchanted, delinquent and engaged in criminality.[55] Masta Lius flocked to join the militia groups in 1999–2000, finding therein an otherwise lacking sense of purpose and direction (a factor that also helps to explain their reluctance to surrender their guns). Similar urbanised or peri-urbanised younger generations exist in Vanuatu and PNG.[56] In western Melanesia, economic weakness and poor governance are closely interrelated. Once the downward spiral commences, the propensity is to fall back on the *wantok* system. The broader ethnic identities, used for mobilisation, may be relatively fluid, and assume new or hitherto unfamiliar shapes and forms.

Are Solomon Islands-type frictions culminating in state failure likely to be replicated across the region? This is unlikely for several reasons. First, resentment against non-indigene preponderance in the capital, Honiara, was particularly intense on Guadalcanal. Honiara's population doubled in the decade after independence (1978–88) and by 1986 first-generation incomers comprised 65% of the town's population. 'Temporary Occupation Licenses' allowed sizeable squatter settlements to develop on government-owned lands around the capital. The 1986 census found that rural Guadalcanal-born citizens made up less than 5 per cent of Honiara's population.[57] Malaitans also predominated in Honiara-based civil service employment and accounted, ominously, for around 75 per cent of the Solomon Islands Police Force.[58] In most other parts of the Pacific, indigenous exclusion from the capital city has not been so extreme.

Second, Guadalcanal's internal migration pattern was unusual and did not solely involve a periphery to metropolis movement, but also interisland movement to rural areas. The fertile northern plains, Honiara's breadbasket, became a major focus for Malaitan inward migration, as did the north-west of the island. Some migrants married into local lineages or established close and durable links with village elders. Others resided in separate Malaitan villages or worked as employees for Solomon Islands Plantations Ltd (SIPL), which ran the large palm oil estates to the east of Henderson Airport. Two thirds of the SIPL workforce was Malaitan, and the larger towns on the northern plains were all company housing estates occupied by migrant workers and their kith and kin. The Gold Ridge mine in the Guadalcanal interior, which commenced operations in 1998, had a majority Malaitan workforce, as did the rice projects at Metapona and Aruligo, Pacific Timbers at Foxwood and the Russell Islands Plantation Estate Ltd (RIPEL) copra estates at Tenaru and Lungga. The GRA/IFM was not able to evict migrants from the capital, but it was capable of chasing them from more isolated rural homesteads.

Third, the crisis on Guadalcanal arose after at least a decade of irresponsible and corrupt government associated with the log export boom of the 1990s.[59] The grievances expressed by Solomon Islanders, particularly from Guadalcanal and the Western Province, had long festered. Demands for state government and restrictions on internal migration had, for example, already been a major issue during the 1987 constitutional review.[60] Ironically, as in Fiji, it was the election of a reformist government that triggered the emergence of an insurgent movement that, in many respects, was mounting a challenge against decades of postcolonial mismanagement.

Petri-dish scenarios aside, the justifications for Australia's intervention along the arc of instability appear to be specific to the Solomons. It is unlikely that the doctrine of 'cooperative intervention' could be replicated across the Pacific. Neither Fiji nor Papua New Guinea would be likely to provide a Solomons-like 'clear and unambiguous act of consent' for a similar 'substantial and sustained intrusion on their sovereignty'.[61] Without consent, the Pacific Islands Forum would be unlikely to back Australian intervention. As currently formulated, the new doctrine would seem incapable of carrying on its shoulders the heavier load of a broader change in Australia's Pacific policy.

Even when confined to the Solomon Islands, important questions need to be addressed. The lack of a clear purpose is shown, for example, in the frequently heard comments from Australian think tanks that there can be 'no "exit strategy" as far as the neighbourhood is concerned'.[62] The ASPI pamphlet proposes Australian intervention because the Solomon Islands 'probably' cannot turn itself around independently. That may well be true, but it only raises a further issue, unless Australia is prepared to assume responsibility over the much longer haul. The assumption is that the country *will* be able to turn itself around *after* a period of sustained antipodean intervention. The Solomon Islands is to be transported back to the twilight of colonial rule, when colonists wrestled with the problem of developing suitable constitutions and nurturing responsible leaders. Yet foreign intervention has seldom proved an effective catalyst for strengthening indigenous democracy. Post-Dayton Bosnia, which is upheld as a model by the ASPI, saw international authorities increasingly embroiled, even in the management of local municipal councils.[63]

Notes

1   I am indebted to Hugh Laracy for the phrase 'matrix of discontent' (see 'Ocean of Peace now a Matrix of Discontent', *Australian*, 7 June 2000).
2   M. Maher, 'Islands in the Storm', *Bulletin*, 20 June 2000; B. Reilly, 'Internal Conflict and Regional Security in Island Asia: Stabilizing the "Arc of Instability"' in B. Vaughn (ed), *The Unravelling of Island Asia? Government, Communal and Regional Instability* (London, Praeger, 2002); Robert Barwick, 'Arc of Instability; Australia is surrounded by an arc of crisis hotspots that are all of its own making', *Australian Dossier*, 14 June 2000.
3   'Asia-Pacific Arc of Instability', Kevin Clements and Ed Garcia of International Alert and APPRA (Asia-Pacific Peace Research Association) 8–10 December 2001, Maryridge, Tagaytay City, Philippines.
4   'The Eye of the Storm: Northern Australia's Location in an arc of instability', Charles Darwin Symposium Series, 29–30 September 2003, Northern Territory University (see ntu.edu.au/cdss2003/cdss_s3_p3.html).
5   '. . . Military planners are talking about establishing semi-permanent or permanent bases along a giant swathe of global territory—increasingly referred to as the "arc of instability", from the Caribbean Basin through Africa to South and Central Asia and across to North Korea' (Jim Lobe, 'Pentagon Moving Swiftly to become "Globocop"', Silver City, NM and Washington, DC, *Foreign Policy in Focus*, 12 June 2003); 'an "arc of instability". . . ranges from the Balkans and West Africa through the Middle East to South and Southeast Asia' ('In the Shadow of War: Iraq, Israel and Palestine', *Middle East Report*, 225 (2002); 'What defence officials call an "arc of instability". . . runs from the Andean region in the Southern Hemisphere through North Africa to the Middle East and into Southeast Asia' (Vernon Loeb, 'New Bases Reflect Shift in Military', *Washington Post*, 9 June 2003; see also Scott Peterson, 'Arc of Instability; Central Asia's Islamicist Crucible', *Christian Science Monitor*, 28 November 2000.
6   The Australian Broadcasting Corporation credits Professor Brij Lal with coining the expression (*Lateline*, 5 June 2000, abc.net.au/lateline/archives/s136196.htm), but Paul Dibb used the expression earlier, prior to the Fiji and Solomon Islands coups ('Defending Australia: The Strategic Environment in the Asia-Pacific Region' in R.D. Blackwell and P. Dibb (eds), *America's Asian Alliances* (Cambridge, MA, MIT Press, 2000), p.12. The phrase was knocking around the coffee rooms at ANU in the aftermath of the East Asian financial crisis (personal communications, Professor Ross Garnaut and Graeme Dobbell).
7   Lobe, 'Pentagon Moving'; 'If the US adopts the "*axis of evil*" as its slogan, the EU's equivalent is the "*arc of instability*" on its eastern and southern borders. These two images, and the policy mechanisms they imply, are so very different. One is aggressive and categorical, the other apprehensive and cautious' (Centre for European Policy Studies, 'From arc of evil to axis of instability', Background Notes for the CEPS International Advisory Council, 22 February 2002, www.ceps.be/2002/EmersonIAC.php). Just a week before Fiji's takeover of parliament on 19 May 2000, Russian President Vladimir Putin pointed out that 'an arc of instability has emerged in the republics on Russia's doorstep', *Uzbekistan Weekly News*, 13–20 May 2000.
8   'In the vast Greater Middle East are several arcs of instability, not just one. The most obvious arc follows the historical "Fertile Crescent", from the Nile Valley along the Mediterranean coast through Lebanon and Syria into Mesopotamia and the northern Persian Gulf. Two other arcs are notably unstable, one running from Turkey through the Caucasus to Iran, the other from Iran through Afghanistan and Pakistan to India' ('Arcs of Instability: US Relations in the Greater Middle East', nwc.navy.mil/press/Review/2002/summer/art2-su2.htm). Another

possibility is that the geopolitical concept was earlier adapted from an expression describing the instability exhibited by the arc of a xenon lamp (see http://www.ltilamps.com/techinfo/arc_instab.html).

9   http://www.nato.int/docu/speech/1998/s980526a.htm. General Naumann had previously used the expression in the early 1990s when Chief of Defence in Germany (personal communication, on behalf of General Naumann, from his former Chief of Cabinet at NATO, Colonel Gerd Bischof, 14 July 2003).

10 worldvision.org/worldvision/pr.nsf/stable/991221_gh; J. Feffer and K. Lee, 'The Northeast Asian Arc of Crisis', *Peacework*, October 1999, afsc.org.pwork/1099/1010.htm; A. Reding, 'Latin America's "Arc of Crisis"', Pacific News Service, 30 May 2000, pacificnews.org/jinn/6.11/000530-crisis.html.

11 See G. Lenczowski, 'The Arc of Crisis: Its Central Sector', *Foreign Affairs* (Spring,1979); Fred Halliday, *Soviet Policy in the Arc of Crisis* (Washington, Institute for Policy Studies, 1981).

12 'International Relations', *Encyclopaedia Brittanica*, 2003, Encyclopaedia Britannica Premium Service, accessed 7 July 2003, http://www.britannica.com/eb/article?eu=108379.

13 G. Sheridan, 'Breaking up brings no benefit: We are witnessing the Balkanisation of the region', *Australian*, 9 June 2000.

14 'The copy-cat coup', *Sydney Morning Herald*, 6 June 2000; M. O'Callaghan, 'Solomons' Copycat Coup', *Australian*, 6 June 2000; Greg Ansley and Bronwyn Sell, 'Copycat coup Waiting to Happen', *New Zealand Herald Online*, 12 June 2000; B. Reilly, 'The Africanisation of the Pacific', *Australian Journal of International Affairs*, 54, 3 (2000), p.262; for a critique of the Africanisation thesis, see J. Fraenkel, 'The Coming Anarchy in Oceania? A Critique of the "Africanisation of the South Pacific" Thesis', *Journal of Commonwealth and Comparative Politics*, 42, 1 (2004).

15 S. Windybank and M. Manning, 'Papua New Guinea on the Brink', *Issue Analysis*, 30 March 2003, Centre for Independent Studies.

16 Helen Hughes, 'Aid has failed the Pacific', *Issue Analysis*, 33, Centre for Independent Studies, pp.3, 12.

17 Australian Strategic Policy Institute, *Our Failing Neighbour: Australia and the Future of the Solomon Islands*, p.13.

18 'Solomons Mission ushers in New Role', *Australian*, 2 July 2003.

19 Cited in Mary-Louise O'Callaghan, 'Australians arrive in Solomons', *Australian*, 2 July 2003 (my emphasis). For Mr Downer, this was a striking *volte* face. In January 2003, he had argued that 'sending in Australian troops to occupy the Solomon Islands would be folly in the extreme' and that 'it would not work, no matter how it was dressed up' (A. Downer, 'No Quick Fix for Troubled Solomons', *Australian*, 8 January 2003).

20 Downer, cited in 'Solomons Mission ushers in new role', *Australian*, 2 July 2003; ASPI, 'Our Failing Neighbour', p.52. The two conditions successfully insisted upon by Canberra were 'a clear and formal request from the Solomons and the passage of legislation by the Solomons parliament' ('Solomons' Formal Plea for Help given Wings', Mary-Louise O'Callaghan, *Australian*, 5 July 2003).

21 On the reasons for reluctance to accept French assistance from nearby New Caledonia, see 'French Role in Solomons seen as Sensitive', *ABC News Online*, 3 July 2003.

22 R. Crocombe, 'Enhancing Pacific Security', Forum Regional Security Committee (FRSC) Meeting, Port Vila, Vanuatu, 13–15 July 2000, p.3; Crocombe et al, 'Security in Melanesia:

Fiji, Papua New Guinea, Solomon Islands and Vanuatu', Pacific Islands Forum Secretariat, Forum Regional Security Meeting, 25–26 June 2001, May 2001; S. Firth, 'Conceptualising Security in Oceania; New and Enduring Issues', *Security in Oceania in the 21st Century*, Asia-Pacific Centre for Security Studies, 2003; Biketawa Declaration, 28 October 2000.

23 Michael Field, 'South Pacific Security Authorities Quietly Close Down Possible al-Qaeda Operation', Agence France-Presse (AFP), 28 April 2003.

24 See *Islands Business*, July 2003; 'Muslim Infiltrators Training Papuan Militia', *Sydney Morning Herald*, 22 January 2002; 'Tongans deny al-Qaeda Shipping Ties', *Radio Australia*, 10 January 2003; 'Greece traces route of seized ship', Cable News Network (CNN), 24 June 2003; 'Captain says ship's owner ordered halt in Greece', *International Herald Tribune*, 26 June 2003; 'US cited Tonga as Potential Nest for Terrorists', *Radio Australia*, 3 January 2003; 'Nauru to End Offshore Banking under US Pressure', Pacific Islands News Agency (PINA), 2 March 2003.

25 Radio New Zealand, 4 July 2003, as reported by John Henderson, 'Island State Security in the post 9/11 World: New Agendas or Priorities?', *Island-State Security 2003: Oceania at the Crossroads*, Asia-Pacific Centre for Security Studies, 15–17 July 2003.

26 Guadalcanal, Western Province, Choiseul, Makira, Temotu and Rennell and Bellona.

27 Townsville Peace Agreement, 15 October 2000, part 4, 1(b).

28 The situation in the Solomon Islands was predicted for some time,' Rabuka told *Australian* on 8 June, 'intelligence had been received by the police and the prime minister's office that there was a coup in the making' (cited Robert Barwick, 'Arc of Instability; Australia is surrounded by an arc of crisis hotspots that are all of its own making', *Australian Dossier*, 14 June 2000).

29 *Hon Bartholomew Ulfa'alu-V-Attorney-General & Hon. Mannaseh Sogavare & Hon Charles Dausebea & Andrew Nori & members of the Joint Malaita Eagle Force/Paramilitary Force*, High Court of the Solomon Islands, Civil Case (constitutional) number 195 of 2000, Judgement 9 November 2001.

30 Philip Alpers and Conor Twyford, 'Small Arms in the Pacific', Small Arms Survey, Occasional paper No 8, March 2003; D. Hegarty, 'Small Arms in Post-Conflict Situations—Solomon Islands', paper presented at the Pacific Islands Forum Small Arms Workshop, 9–11 May 2001, http://rspas.anu.edu.au/melanesia/workingpaperhegarty01_5.htm, accessed 30 July 2003.

31 'Wantok' is a pidgin expression for people who speak the same language (literally, 'one-talk'), but is more flexibly used to convey kinship, clan or less formal forms of association.

32 Calculated from Central Bank of the Solomon Islands, Annual Report, 2002, Rick Hou 'The Solomon Islands Economy: Recent Developments & the Impact of Ethnic Tensions', *Pacific Economic Bulletin*, 17, 2 (2002), table 1, p.17. For a more detailed investigation of the Solomon Islands crisis, see J. Fraenkel, *The Manipulation of Custom; From Uprising to Intervention in the Solomon Islands* (Wellington and Canberra, Victoria University Press and Pandanus Books, 2004).

33 J. Fraenkel, 'The Alternative Vote System in Fiji: Electoral Engineering or Ballot-rigging', *Journal of Commonwealth & Comparative Politics*, 39, 2 (2001).

34 Speight was eventually arrested and imprisoned for life on charges of high treason. For a more detailed account of the Fiji 2000 crisis, see J. Fraenkel, 'The Clash of Dynasties and the Rise of Demagogues: Fiji's *Tauri Vakaukauwa* of May 2000', *Journal of Pacific History*, 35, 3 (2000).

35 See George Williams, 'The Case that Stopped a Coup? The Rule of Law and Constitutionalism in Fiji', *Oxford University Commonwealth Law Journal*, 1 (2001); Michael Head, 'A Victory for Democracy? An Alternative Assessment of *Republic of Fiji V Prasad*', *Melbourne Journal of International Law*, 2 (2001); Justice K.R. Handley, 'The Constitutional Crisis in Fiji', *Australian Law Journal*, 75 (2001).

36 United Nations Electoral Observer Mission for the General Elections in Fiji in August 2001, 'Report of the Secretary General, UN General Assembly', 10 November 2001; 'Fiji Islands General Election' 25 August to 5 September 2001, Report of the Commonwealth Observer Group, Commonwealth Secretariat, London. 2001.

37 Court of Appeal (2001) *Chaudhry V Qarase, President & Attorney General*, Civil Action No 282 of 2001, Misc 1/2001; Supreme Court. (2003). *Qarase V Chaudhry*, Civil Appeal No. CBV 0004 of 2002S, 18 July 2003.

38 New Zealand High Commissioner to Tonga, Brian Smythe, Nuku'alofa, to Phil Goff, Minister for Foreign Affairs and Trade, September 2001, leaked to *New Zealand Herald*, 11 June 2003.

39 Scott Whitney, 'Watery Continent or Invisible Lake? US pays little Attention to Asia—but less to the Pacific', *Pacific Magazine*, June 2003.

40 See, for example, 'Tongan Crown Prince slams Singaporeans and own subjects', *Pacific Islands Report*, 3 January 2000.

41 With the exception of French Polynesia, Hawaii, Palau and the Federated States of Micronesia

42 Anthropologists will rightly respond that this distinction is often overplayed, pointing for example to more centralised polities amongst the Kanaks of New Caledonia. Exceptions aside, however, the contrast is sufficiently real to become a topic of political discourse in Fiji, which straddles Polynesia to its west and Melanesia to its east. The power struggle between 1987 coup leader, former prime minister and 'commoner', Sitiveni Rabuka, and former president, *Tui Nayau* and *Tui Lau*, Ratu Sir Kamisese Mara, played a critical role in Fiji's politics during the late 1980s and 1990s and a so-far insufficiently documented role at the 1999 polls. It was a conflict depicted by Rabuka himself as one between the more Melanesian model of achievement-based leadership and the more Polynesian hierarchical conception of hereditary rule.

43 J. Steeves, 'Unbounded Politics in the Solomon Islands: Leadership and Party Alignments', *Pacific Studies*, 19, 1 (1996).

44 Eight of which occurred during the suppression of a mutiny at the military's Queen Elizabeth Barracks on 2 November 2000.

45 The challenge to Indo-Fijian citizenship rights, although never entirely explicit as a campaign stance, peaked with the Fijian Nationalist Party at the April 1977 polls, when it obtained 25 per cent of the indigenous Fijian vote. This has never been, as electorally expressed, the mainstream ethnic Fijian standpoint.

46 P. Collier, 'Economic Causes of Civil Conflict and their Implications for Policy', World Bank, 2000, p.6, http://econ.worldbank.org/files/13198_EcCausesPolicy.pdf.

47 G. Fry, 'Political Legitimacy and the Post-Colonial State in the Pacific: Reflections on Some Common Threads in the Fiji and Solomon Islands Coups', *Pacifica Review*, 12, 3 (2000), p.303.

48 Of the 409,042 people recorded at the 1999 census, 60,275 lived on rural Guadalcanal (14.7

per cent), 49,107 in Honiara (12 per cent) and 122,620 on Maliata (30 per cent). Of course some of these would have been from other islands, and there were some Guadalcanalese and, particularly, Malaitans on other islands. But these additions and subtractions would be unlikely to sizeably change the 56.7 per cent combined figure. The 1999 census, it should be noted, was taken in the midst of the troubles on Guadalcanal (Solomon Island Government, 'Report on the 1999 Population & Housing Census', 1999).

49 M. Esman, *Ethnic Politics* (New York, Cornell University Press, 1994), p.15.
50 W. Davenport and G. Coker, 'The Moro Movement of Guadalcanal, British Solomon Islands protectorate', *Journal of the Polynesian Society*, 76, 2 (1967), pp.123–75, 138.
51 Nick Maclellan, 'New Caledonia Ethnic Strife called Political', *Radio Australia*, 3 July 2003 (reproduced Pacific Islands Report, 4 July 2003).
52 A.L. Epstein, *Ethos and Identity: Three Studies in Ethnicity* (London, Tavistock Publications and Chicago, Aldine Publishing Co, 1978).
53 G.W. Trompf, *Payback: The Logic of Retribution in Melanesian Religions* (Cambridge, Cambridge University Press, 1994).
54 For PNG, see S. Dinnen, 'In Weakness and in Strength—State, Society and Order in Papua New Guinea' in P. Dauvergne (ed), *Weak & Strong States in Asia-Pacific Societies* (Sydney, Allen and Unwin, 1998) UN, Common Country Assessment: Solomon Islands, Suva, Fiji, March 2002, p.29; for Fiji, see D. Forsyth, 'Economy of Fiji' in B.V. Lal and T.R. Vakatora (ed), *Fiji in Transition*, Fiji Constitutional Review Research Papers, vol 1 (Suva, University of the South Pacific, 1997), p.180; for Vanuatu, see S. Chand, and R. Duncan, 'The Economics of the "Arc of Instability"', *Asian-Pacific Economic Literature*, 16, 1 (2002), p.2.
55 Christine Jourdan, 'Masta Liu' in Vered Amit Talai and Helena Wulff (eds), *Youth Cultures: A Cross Cultural Perspective* (New York, Routledge, 1995), pp.202–22.
56 John Connell and John Lea, *Urbanisation in the South Pacific: Towards Sustainable Development* (London and New York, Routledge, 2002), p.94.
57 K. Groenewegen, *Report on the Census of Population*, 1986, Section 2b, Statistics Office, Ministry of Finance, Honiara, 1989, tables IV.3 and IV.4. The 1986 census was the last precrisis census that provides such data. The November 1999 census enumerated Honiara residents after the first wave of crisis-induced displacement.
58 Amnesty International, 'The Solomon Islands: A Forgotten Conflict', August 2000.
59 See J. A. Bennett, *Pacific Forest: A History of Resource Control and Contest in Solomon Islands, c.1800–1997* (Cambridge, White Horse Press, 2000), pp.379–83.
60 See, M. Chapman, 'Population Movement: Free or Constrained?' in R. Crocombe and E. Tuza, *Independence, Dependence, Inter-dependence: The First Ten Years of Solomon Islands Independence* (Honiara, Government Printing Press, 1992), pp.94–5.
61 ASPI, 'Our Failing Neighbour', p.52.
62 S. Windybank and M. Manning, 'Papua New Guinea on the Brink', *Issue Analysis*, 30 (March 2003), p.1; Hugh White, Director ASPI, cited in R. Callick, 'Australia Rethinks the Pacific; Regional Instability, Frustrations Challenge Canberra', *Pacific Magazine*, May 2003.
63 D. Chandler, *Bosnia: Faking Democracy after Dayton* (London, Pluto Press, 1999).

TRANS-TASMAN RELATIONS

11

LOOKING OUT FROM DOWN UNDER: DIVERGING WORLD VIEWS

Terence O'Brien

The pace and intensity of globalisation is shaping the perceptions of governments about what is desirable, or attainable, by way of organising a just and prosperous world. Each country's perception of the world, and of its own place in that world, is derived from its own distinctive geography, history, culture, ambition and resource endowment. Even at a time in history when regionalism is a prevailing feature of the way countries are choosing to organise themselves collectively, disagreements between regional partners can be conspicuous. One lesson of global dynamics is that to be interconnected does not necessarily mean to be harmonious, nor in conformity with a shared single view on the world.

There is nothing so special about the trans-Tasman relationship that renders it immune to these wider international experiences. There are a host of countries, variously connected by history, geography, culture, economics, alliances and ethnicity, that are unequal in size, and whose world views contrast one with another. Malaysia and Singapore, Brunei and Indonesia, Ireland and Britain, Norway and Germany, Finland and Russia, Canada and the US are but just some examples. At a time when there is much debate over the requirements for a just order in the world, differences of view divide countries with otherwise close ties; as the agony over Iraq demonstrates.

New Zealand is in fact a great deal more reticent than Australia about revealing, or explaining, its world view. Australia is one of very few countries that publishes White Papers on foreign policy. In a rapidly changing international context there must always be an element of doubt over the shelf life for such documents. The level of analysis is perhaps for this reason wanting. In conjunction, however, with regular defence policy assessments, they provide the contours for Australia's world view.

US relationship and multilateralism

The 2003 version[1] exudes an air of official confidence in an open, stable Australia that has positioned itself strategically for future prosperity and security, in particular through strengthening links with the US that are judged essential to advancing Australian interests yet further. What makes the US such an attractive and vital partner for Australia, the document makes clear, is America's unchallengeable power, which the authors contend both protects Australia and enhances its voice and influence particularly in Asia.[2] The relationship, in other words, bestows prestige as well as protection. It adds dimension to vital Australian national interests, which now include the nurturing of US credibility in the world.[3]

The strategic commitment therefore confers upon Australia the role of advocate and understudy for America's world view. This can produce effusion. The Australian foreign minister has, for example, accused those critics of the present US administration's unilateralist instincts of 'willfully misrepresenting' America's commitment to an option of pre-emptive military strike, and acting alone if necessary,[4] even when the actual language of Washington's own 2002 National Security Doctrine states the commitment in those terms.

As Australia's commitment to the United States (US), and to upholding American credibility, has deepened, so evidence of a parallel decline in a commitment to the credibility to the United Nations (UN) and the multilateral system of law and order has appeared. The 2003 White Paper acknowledges the UN as a means to pursue practical solutions to transboundary problems, but the foreign minister has dismissed multilateralism as ineffective and unfocused, suggesting Australia has neither the time nor inclination to pursue issues or opportunities that are marginal to Australian interests.[5] His New Zealand counterpart by contrast has insisted it is simply a contradiction to choose selectively which parts of international law are convenient and which are not.[6]

The Australian disdain shared with the US about multilateralism is evident in scepticism over arms control negations under the UN, sustainable environmental management under the Kyoto Protocol, and the need for UN Security Council (UNSC) authorisation of the invasions of Iraq. In all cases as well as others, such as the justification for a strategic missile defence programme and the Proliferation Security Initiative (PSI) involving high-seas interdiction of suspected dangerous arms cargoes from dubious states, Canberra has followed Washington closely. On Iraq, Australia's official rhetoric has implied that those countries (like New Zealand), which maintained the indispensability of UNSC authorisation for an attack, were simply displaying anti-Americanism.

New Zealand perspectives

To track down expressions of New Zealand's world view requires a traverse through a thicket of ministerial speeches and similar documents to glean evidence of the components for such a view. One approximation was an analysis in 2000 of foreign and security policy challenges confronting the country.[7] There is of course more to a world view than the defence security dimension alone. And since publication of that document momentous events have anyway overtaken the world, especially the eruption of international terror which grievously impacted Australia. But there are some markers there that would seem to have been validated by what has transpired since.

The document avers that it is an acceptable position for New Zealand to be a friend and not an ally of the US. It acknowledges the profound influence that the US has over New Zealand and the natural affinity of interest on many issues, although the way in which the US exercises its immense influence will not necessarily always accord with New Zealand interests or perceptions. It urges a good working relationship with the US especially on defence, and the need to make common cause where and when possible.

In its discussion of the Australian relationship, the document highlights certain challenges for New Zealand including the absolute primacy attached by Australia to its military alliance with the US. It says that Australia's 'middle power' ambition gives rise to a tendency to overlook the interests of small neighbours and that Australia has, by tradition, a significantly more negative assessment of the security outlook. The document also highlights the centrality of the defence and security relationship amongst the many strands of the trans-Tasman connection and, of course, differences over nuclear policy.

As the smaller partner, New Zealand resists the notion that any one dimension should become the touchstone for the total trans-Tasman relationship. The extent of integration achieved under the 1983 Closer Economic Relations (CER) agreement has been a notable advantage to both countries. The very extent of the integration, however, exposes the absence of common or convergent economic and social policy making and the actual constraint this imposes upon further integration. Although there have been proposals from non-government sources inside New Zealand for a European Union (EU) type of association with Australia and some economists have called for establishment of a single currency, proposals from New Zealand policy advisers have traditionally stopped short (in areas such as fiscal, tax or monetary policy) of any ideas involving issues of New Zealand sovereignty.[8]

The closeness of economic interests has, however, provided the foundation for a shared world view about international economic issues, especially trade. Australia's leadership of the Cairns Group on liberalisation of international farm trade has been valuable to New Zealand. With the uncertainties surrounding further liberalisation of world trade under the World Trade Organisation (WTO) in 2002–03 both counties have sought bilateral trade agreements with other partners—a move that could potentially affect the trans-Tasman economic connection. The attempt to lever the CER agreement as the basis for a free-trade agreement in South-East Asia with the Association of South East Asian Nations (ASEAN) has not been crowned with success for political as much as economic reasons. These are covered in later sections of this chapter dealing with Australia's uneasy political relations in East Asia.

New Zealand's foreign policy remains deeply grounded in the small country tradition. Its statecraft asserts the rule of law and the importance of a balance of interests between countries. It supports international institutions, conference diplomacy, cooperative not competitive management of security, equality between states and international negotiation with agendas and outcomes that are fair to all involved. It is committed to a reputation for good global citizenship through the provision of support, including military support, to nation building in the world. By definition, it is non-threatening, with an aptitude for impartiality and problem solving. New Zealand and Australia share many values but not the same attributes nor ambitions. New Zealand does not seek international prestige as Australia does.

There is more to the substance of a world view, than strategic perceptions alone, although such perceptions are a significant ingredient for a world view. Geography is the key. Australia's size, her potential and her physical proximity to Asia are critical strategic factors which account for the paradox between Australia's sense of confidence and her sense of insecurity. Together these factors drive foreign and security policy respectively. New Zealand's different geography, size and potential in the same way shape its strategic perceptions, and a sense of comparative security. In a wired world of deepening interdependence, New Zealand's discrete geographical location provides the protection of a moat from globalising scourges including terrorism and environmental degradation. New Zealand is not isolationist. With innovative policy governments can fashion New Zealand's geographical situation into strategic advantage although not every New Zealand official necessarily shares this upbeat perspective. In 2003 the Ministry of Foreign Affairs and Trade (MFAT) expressed to the New Zealand government its opinion that 'the real limitations of a small, isolated country in a highly competitive world breed concerns about the risks of marginalisation'.[9] This prosaic sentiment contrasts with the more confident rhetoric of the Australian White Paper on foreign policy.

There seems no doubt that the earlier traditional idea that New Zealand and Australia possess a set of more or less identical strategic objectives and interests has receded as a realisation has grown that differences in physical and political geography legitimately determine the way that New Zealand, and Australia, think about security.[10] This realisation perhaps came a little later in Australia where publicly disparaging attitudes about New Zealand's defence effort, its nuclear policy and its perceived absence of real strategic understanding persist. The New Zealand decision not to join the 2003 US-led invasion of Iraq rekindled asperity. Officially, however, Australia describes its partnership with New Zealand as of 'first order importance' emphasising that both countries should respect each other as sovereign nations acting reasonably and properly in accordance with their respective national interests.[11]

Nonetheless the depth and quality of analysis by Canberra, that lies behind the way policy positions are fashioned, does reflect Australia's world view. In Australia the realist tradition derived from Anglo-American strategic security thinking is strong. Realism has its place, although as a theory for explaining the modern interdependent world it has definite limitations. In that tradition, however, small countries are a problem for the more powerful. They are vulnerable, they free-ride on the security and prosperity of the more powerful, they complicate the task of collective decision making, and they perversely assert their identity by adopting policies that deliberately differ from the preferences of the more powerful.

This realist thinking colours Australian perceptions in the Pacific Islands region. But more importantly, it clearly infuses their views about New Zealand. Among the charmed circle of specialists, commentators and media that orbit the Canberra political-security community, enduring criticism of New Zealand reflects the trite and facile small country stereotyping of realism. There is an unquestioned presumption that New Zealand's world view should duplicate Australia's vision, although such attitudes have moderated in some significant respects. The result is misperception on both sides of the Tasman. New Zealand recalibrates its defence efforts to produce a small mobile expeditionary-force capability, while critics in Australia judge that New Zealand is walking away from responsibilities and commitments and disregarding Australian interests. New Zealand believes that it can best contribute to world order at a time of notable internal disruption globally through peace building, preferably under the UN. To do this it needs a professional force that displays aptitude for the dangerous task of peace support. Australian critics consider New Zealand is reducing its capacities by concentrating on activities that are not the 'real stuff' of high security. These critics consider that New Zealand's defence capabilities are weakened by its inability to exercise or train with the US which, because of incompatibility over nuclear policy, refuses such opportunities to New Zealand. Australia itself has sternly insisted in Washington that the US not relax retribution for New Zealand's non-nuclear policy.[12] It is relevant here that joint exercises with friends, as well as with allies, is now a prevailing feature of existing US defence policy.

The watershed for existing trans-Tasman misperception remains the 1985 New Zealand non-nuclear policy which has virtually ensured that the trans-Tasman partners will have a differing world view. For many in Australia, and some still in New Zealand, the policy represents a flagrant disregard of Australia's interests, and a wholly perverse exhibition of wrong-headed nationalism on New Zealand's part.[13] Non-nuclear policy in today's world is in fact a bolder and even-handed version of non-proliferation policy. Non-proliferation is of course, the crucial preoccupation of the international community. Even two decades later, however, a view persists in Australia, and in some quarters in New Zealand, that as a result of the policy New Zealand has lost its way and its self-confidence.[14] Yet there is, quite to the contrary, solid evidence to support a view that over the period New Zealand has made measurable progress politically, economically and socially and in the process is defining an international identity with confidence.[15] Above all, New Zealand has had the self-belief to pursue within its own society the immensely challenging goal of reconciliation, a goal that Australia is not able or ready to emulate.

Asia and Pacific

The realities of the trans-Tasman relationship are such that New Zealand has a vested interest in the success and effectiveness of Australian foreign policy in its Pacific neighbourhood and in East Asia. Setbacks to Australia, or clumsy performance by Australia, rebounds to New Zealand's disadvantage. Differences between perception and reality are important in international affairs. The 2003 Australian foreign policy White Paper confidently paints a reassuring image for Australia about the quality of its relationships in Asia, because of the skill and effectiveness of its diplomacy and the advantages conferred by the affinity with the US. Australian success in negotiating new economic agreements with Thailand and Singapore, and its huge 2003 liquid gas contract with China, provide measurable proof. There is, however, credible evidence that points to a widening gap between Australian self-perceptions of its ties in Asia, and the reality of how Australia is actually regarded by several regional countries.[16]

Widespread rebuke from South-East Asian capitals over the notion that Australia should serve as the US understudy in East Asia (the so-called deputy sheriff role) indicates that the strength and nature of Australia's alliance with the US actually provides a complication. Even East Asian governments who themselves have active defence ties with the US joined the chorus of disapproval about the idea of deputy sheriff. Similar reactions greeted the Australian prime minister's reported avowal that Australia might itself strike pre-emptively against terrorist threats under preparation in South-East Asia against Australia. Indonesia has, moreover, clearly indicated that national cohesion, and not terrorism, remains its number one security preoccupation.

New Zealand cannot entirely ignore the implications of accusations from within the region criticising Australia's arrogance, condescension, capacity for interference, double standards on human rights and poor record in respect to its own indigenous people. It is important of course to see such criticism for what it sometimes is, opportunistic scapegoating designed to keep Australia on the back foot.[17] There is a sense at times, that is quite right and proper for regional leaders to criticise Australia, but not for Australia to criticise South-East Asia in return.

Indonesia is a particular case in point. The 1999 East Timor intervention led by Australia, whilst conspicuously successful in achieving its ends, had a particularly abrasive impact upon relations between the countries. At the same time the 2002 Bali bombing created deep anguish for Australia, a factor that New Zealand for its part needs to bear closely in mind. Australia's relations with Jakarta will continue to be sensitive, especially as Australia re-equips its defence forces with technologically advanced fighter aircraft, longer-range offensive missiles, Airborne Warning and Control Systems (AWACS), and battle tanks in the years immediately ahead. The close alliance with the US obliges Australia to keep pace with the US in military capability and to bear substantial financial cost. It means seriously examining Australian involvement in the controversial US missile defence system. The actual Australian threat assessment that rationalises the new defence policy and the new capital acquisitions will be studied carefully in Jakarta and other capitals to determine what greater military edge they bestow upon Australia over South-East Asia. They cannot be explained as a response to international terrorism. The retention of a military edge has been a long-standing Australian defence objective and a durable source therefore of potential regional friction.

The depleted condition of Australia's relations in parts of East Asia helps explain the adamant exclusion of Australia, and by extension New Zealand, from association with the newly emerging regional arrangements under consideration, or already in place, like ASEAN Plus Three and the Asia-Europe Meeting (ASEM). There is sense that the East Asian region is itself at the threshold of significant change institutionally although progress may not necessarily be swift. Australia has made clear its desire for involvement. Some of its diplomacy, according to anecdotal evidence, has been robust. New Zealand, again according to anecdote, considers such robustness unwise and an example of Canberra's capacity for exaggerating Australia's influence in the region; with consequences that are negative, by extension, for New Zealand which prefers low-key persistence.

All this does suggest New Zealand needs to be less reticent about explaining and projecting its world view, not in any spirit of competition with Australia, but simply by conveying the facts of its modern situation with a view to underlining to Asian governments that the two countries are intrinsically different. New Zealand should, for example, move to sign ASEAN's Treaty of Amity, even if Australia hesitates. One should not overestimate the challenge to New Zealand. There is no obviously compelling reason for Asian governments to treat the Tasman partners dissimilarly, although given the discrepancy in their size and potential New Zealand interests could be, in theory, the more readily accommodated by

Asian governments if they are convinced by quiet persistence of the utility of doing so.

In the Pacific Australia's world view directly influenced its 2003 decision to lead an intervention force into the Solomon Islands to restore law and order. New Zealand contributed a contingent of police and infantry. This intrusion was a notable departure from established policy practice by both metropolitan countries in the Pacific Island region. The hint was dropped in an announcement by the Australian prime minister, that the Solomons expedition might indeed provide a template for future Australian preemptive action in the Pacific Island region should the need arise.[18]

Australia accepted, or was persuaded to accept, the precondition of a formal request from the Solomon's authorities for assistance to restore law and order, and consequential endorsement of that request from the Pacific Islands Forum. Aside from this admittedly important distinction, Australia's action resembled a cameo of the US-led strike against Iraq without UN Security Council endorsement. Australia saw no requirement for UN approval, a view which New Zealand seemingly accepted. There was, at least in the public domain, a sense of an Australian fait accompli constructed for demonstration effect with the US, offering tangible proof for Washington of Australia's will and capacity to handle Pacific regional instability.[19]

New Zealand and Australia share a deep interest in sustaining a prosperous well-disposed Pacific Island neighbourhood. In contrast to New Zealand, Australian preoccupations at the senior political level with the region have been episodic. Australian prime ministers have quite frequently passed up the annual Pacific Forum Summit of regional leaders. The 2003 Solomons intervention was in fact the product of a sudden reversal of earlier Australian disinterest. If it is a signal of substantive change by Australia, whose menu of other external preoccupations exceeds that of New Zealand, that must be a welcome development. It will, however, oblige both metropolitan governments to consistently share perceptions, to concert diplomacy, and above all to avoid surprises.

The suggestion that the Pacific Islands region displays all the hallmarks, like Africa, of an area of failing states, and that the Solomons is merely a foretaste of things to come, is a judgement that New Zealand does not necessarily share.[20] There is hesitation, moreover, about a prescription for more robust metropolitan supervision including ever-stricter conditionality for aid disbursements. This prescription finds favour now in Australia where the belief persists that unless rapid conversion to free-market reform occurs, instability will worsen.[21] Canberra coined the description 'arc of instability' for the island region to Australia's north. There is an undiscriminating quality to this depiction in the sense that a 'one-size-fits-all' attitude fails as either a prescription or a remedy for such a notably disparate region.

Such differences as exist here between the approaches of New Zealand and Australia to the Pacific Islands region must not be overstated. They are to an important degree, the sort of differences that are the daily menu of diplomatic dealings of governments with shared interests. They require nonetheless careful and consistent management by both parties.

Conclusions

Disagreements over the strategic view between the trans-Tasman partners is hardly new. There were during the twentieth century occasions when differences were acrimonious.[22] The iron law of geography and the sense of shared interest, however, nourished relationship building, notably in the economic area. There were practical steps for closer defence cooperation. There is no divine ordinance, however, that decrees that this will persist without cultivation. Perhaps the greater onus rests upon the smaller partner to take pains to ensure this care is taken. Respect for each other's viewpoints and judgements remains indispensable. This is harder for an ambitious Australia. There is a discernible difference between the Tasman partners over the big issues of peace and justice in the world; with New Zealand espousing the rule of law equitably applied by all states, and Australia pragmatically recognising the rule of invincibility and compliance with the paramount power. Both see their position as the way to provide honourable guarantees of global stability and fairness.

Notes

1 *Advancing the National Interest*, National Capital Printing, Canberra, 2003.
2 J. Camilleri, 'A Leap into the Past in the Name of National Interest', *Australian Journal of International Affairs*, 57, 3 (2003), pp.431–53.
3 Australian Strategic Policy Institute (ASPI), *Building the Peace: Australia and the Future in Iraq* (2003), p.6.
4 Alexander Downer, 'Insight', *Radio New Zealand* interview, 9 November 2003.
5 Alexander Downer, speech to National Press Club, Canberra, 26 June 2003, www.foreignminister.news.com.au.
6 Phil Goff, speech to Australia–New Zealand Society of International Law; 4 July 2003, www.beehive.govt.New Zealand.

7 *New Zealand Foreign and Security Policy Challenge*, Ministry of Foreign Affairs and Trade, June 2000.
8 *Australian Strategy*, Australian Division MFAT, April 2002.
9 *Statement of Intent*, New Zealand MFAT, May 2003, www.mft.govt.nz.
10 H. White, 'Refocusing the Dialogue on Strategic Cooperation', *New Zealand International Review*, 27, 1 (2002), pp.2–4.
11 A. Calvert, 'Australian Foreign Policy Priorities', *New Zealand International Review*, 28, 5 (2003), pp.25–8.
12 D. Mclean, *The Prickly Pair: Making Nationalism in Australia and New Zealand* (Dunedin, Otago University Press, 2003), p.261.
13 D. Mclean, *The Prickly Pair*, pp, 256–7.
14 A. Behm in A. Grimes and L. Wevers (eds), *States of Mind* (Wellington, Institute of Policy Studies Victoria University of Wellington, 2002), pp.95–108.
15 T. O'Brien in *States of Mind*, pp.109–115.
16 A. Broinowski, *About Face* (Carlton North, Scribe Publications, 2003), p.4.
17 A. Broinowski, *About Face*, p.11.
18 G. Sheridan, 'Howard's Revolution on Policy', *Australian*, 25 July 2003, www.theaustralian.news.com.au
19 Australian Strategic Policy Institute (ASPI), *Our Failing Neighbour*, ASPI Policy Report www.aspi.org.au
20 M. Powles, 'Understanding Our Pacific Neighbourhood', *New Zealand International Review*, 28, 6 (2003), pp.2–5.
21 H. Hughes, *Aid has Failed the Pacific*, Issues Analysis for Centre for Independent Studies, 33, 7 (2003), p.25.
22 D. Mclean, *The Prickly Pair*, pp.111–14.

12

BEING ON THE RIGHT SIDE OF HISTORY

Les Holborow

Several recent commentators on New Zealand's foreign policy stance have asked whether our current differences with Australia represent something more fundamental than a disagreement about the merits of particular engagements such as Iraq. Perhaps they are an argument about how much in the way of resources we need to devote to defence and security. Recent presentations in New Zealand by Gerald Henderson, in particular, have raised questions such as—Has New Zealand's government failed to discern the course of history and position our country accordingly? Has New Zealand adjusted appropriately to the post-9/11 world? Have we made a mistake in believing that we can continue as a 'good friend'(even if a 'very, very good friend') of the world's major power without becoming a relatively uncritical alliance partner as Australia has done?

To state the issue more broadly, is there a viable place in world affairs for a small power, such as we are, to be aligned with previous allies, such as the United States (US), Australia and the United Kingdom (UK), but to retain a sufficient degree of independence in our foreign and security policies to be able to choose on a case-by-case basis whether to support particular initiatives and campaigns? Does our doing so effectively contribute to the maintenance of a healthy multilateral system of international diplomacy and dispute-resolution, or does it leave us exposed to the cold winds which can be expected to blow on those not sheltered within the protective walls of the new imperial city?

I consider that this issue is still worth addressing even if it does not now present itself quite as starkly as it appeared to a few months ago. The US, and in particular President Bush, have clearly softened their language since the 'either for us or against us' formulations of the axis of evil speech. The transition from the euphoria of the quick military triumph of the Iraqi main campaign to the messy, difficult and hazardous reality of attempted postwar consolidation has no doubt influenced this. New Zealand's willingness to assist with engineers in Iraq following our commitment of special forces in Afghanistan makes a nonsense of any attempt to regard all non-allies as unhelpful or perverse. Hence the tone of regret rather than recrimination in the US ambassador's recent speech notes, for the address which he nearly gave at Victoria University, on the matter of New Zealand's not joining the Iraqi intervention.

A similar point about the need for nuances can be made with reference to the large power China. Even seen from Washington, China must surely be regarded as a helpful broker with respect to North Korea, a trading partner of much potential in the World Trade Organisation (WTO) negotiations, and a Security Council member whose vote for the recent resolution, exhorting all countries to assist postwar reconstruction in Iraq despite continued American occupation, was valuable.

So the situation is not totally polarised—we are not on the horns of a dilemma. But there is still an issue. There is still a strongly held belief that as long as we stay outside the US/Australia alliance, in particular, both our security and our economic well-being will be increasingly threatened. The argument is that we are in danger of becoming increasingly unable to rely on the cooperation of these major powers in defence and security, and progressively isolated economically as bilateral trade agreements shut us out of favourable opportunities for trade and investment. Speaking at the Stout Centre Trans-Tasman Conference, the doyen of Australian media commentators, Laurie Oakes, traced a growing disinterest in New Zealand in the Australian media to a feeling that our countries were drifting apart in the security area. He conceded that the contribution of New Zealand forces to East Timor had been valuable and effective, but judged that it was not in itself sufficient to dispel the overall impression that Australia could not rely on New Zealand's support as it had in the past.

To begin at the security end of the matter, we need to note that we have cooperated with Australia in the Solomons, though apparently our desire not to move troops until we secured the support of other Pacific nations caused some nervousness in Canberra. We have also worked with the British in Afghanistan, though one hears comment from military circles that our ability to slot in to operations there was severely tested. The claim is made that our inability to join exercises with the US and Australia is having a cumulative effect on our level of expertise. The danger is that we will fall further behind as the US adopts more state-of-the-art technology. There are questions of affordability as well as intensity of training involved here. It seems imperative that New Zealand's armed forces maintain a constantly updated communications capacity and that arrangements are made, particularly with Australia, to hone their expertise in regular exercises. The argument for this must rest not on any claim that we are entitled to freeload on Australia, but rather on the consideration that it is in Australia's interest for reasons of regional security to have New Zealand's armed forces in a state of preparedness for cooperative action. On this basis we are prepared both to meet regional needs and to contribute as we decide is appropriate to wider global peacekeeping or even peace enforcement.

This does not, of course, assume that our two countries must always make the same decision about whether to support any particular intervention by the US or any broader coalition elsewhere. There clearly needs to be a belief that there will be a reliable congruence of interests sufficient to justify the effort involved in cooperative exercises and planning. The increased volatility in the South Pacific provides a core around which such a congruence can be identified. We clearly no longer regard the South Pacific as a benign strategic environment. New Zealand merely needs to avoid any sense that it is the assistant to the US's deputy sheriff. This will be greatly assisted if Australia can manage to avoid attracting that title for its own activities in this region.

Looking more globally, it can be argued that the fact that Australia has decided to be a relatively uncritical supporter of the US makes it all the more important that New Zealand retain the ability to make independent assessments and thus to query at any feasible level any unwise commitments that Australia may be contemplating. This could be in Australia's interests as well as New Zealand's, especially at a time when the political opposition in Australia is relatively weak. It could be expected that other countries in our region would welcome New Zealand's filling this role. It should assist the security debate, in South-East Asia especially, for us to be speaking with an independent voice. On the global scene as well, New Zealand's participation as a small country speaking independently is a contribution to the effective functioning of multilateral institutions, above all the United Nations (UN). Although there was much talk earlier in 2003 (and more recently here from such authoritative figures as Paul Holmes) of the ineffectiveness and even 'failure' of the UN, recent events call for a reassessment. It was seen even by the US as important for them to get a UN resolution legitimising their continued presence in Iraq. The Madrid Donor Conference was important because even the US is finding the costs of funding postwar reconstruction in Iraq a significant budgetary headache. It is salutary to recall the glib talk of rapidly restored oil revenues as providing a copious resource to employ private firms from favoured countries for this task. It is also worth remembering the reports of serious consideration being given to extending the intervention into Iraq to Syria and/or Iran. It is easy, even for a superpower, to be tempted to bite off more than it can chew. Hopefully the realisation is sinking in.

It is also worth noting two other conspicuous areas of international policy where New Zealand clearly benefits from not being closely tied to the US/Australia axis. These are environmental policy and the policy concerning international legal institutions.

While there is much scope for argument about the detail of the Kyoto Protocol, most New Zealanders would surely consider that it is our country rather than the US and Australia which are on the better side of this debate. Many would also refer to New Zealand's antinuclear stance at this point. I would comment that it is interesting to see how far we have been able to carry the argument of this chapter without relying on that consideration.

Similar comments can be made about support for the rule of international law, including the proposed International Criminal Court (ICC). Whereas Australia is compelled to swallow its qualms about its own citizens being subject to arbitrary detention at Guantanamo Bay, New Zealand is free to give its support to the development of the ICC, in common with a large group of other nations. This is a policy position consistent with its support for the development of an international legal order over a long period.

It is not a lonely stance in either of these areas. To mention only two of several other countries, Germany and Canada take a very similar position. If it is not in accord with the course of history, however, then there is indeed reason to worry about the future.

13

A TALE OF TWO NATION-STATES

Damian Edwards[1]

The trans-Tasman relationship has been under renewed scrutiny over the past few years, primarily due to the passing of Australia's centenary of federation in 2001 and the 20th anniversary of Closer Economic Relationship (CER) this year. Sadly, while this has provided some stimulus in the academic community, and among political and other elites on both sides of the Tasman, little of this debate has permeated to the general populations of both countries beyond the occasional flirtation of the mass media, which has generally been based on a superficial and banal exchange of parochial rhetoric.

However, elite-level discussion has often echoed that of an earlier generation—the period of Australian federation. One of the interesting nuances of the Australian constitution, and there are many, is the reference to New Zealand among the former colonies to be included in the proposed Commonwealth of Australia, a proposition never accepted by the former British colony. While some dispute exists regarding the definitive reasoning behind New Zealand's decision to resist the opportunity to be part of the newly formed Commonwealth, two broad categories encapsulate the primary rationale of elite decision making at the time. Firstly, economic imperatives that had driven much of the impetus for Australia to federate did not apply to New Zealand. With established trade and infrastructure mechanisms in place, the appeal of joining a federated Australia for economic purposes was limited. Secondly, and perhaps more importantly, were questions of national identity. Clearly, even in the late 1800s, New Zealanders had an evolving sense of who they were in the international community. By the time of Australian federation New Zealand had established strong, independent links with Britain, had instituted several landmark legislative initiatives, and had a clear vision of its role in the Pacific region.

Such historical revisionism provides an interesting backdrop to the recent reinvigoration of trans-Tasman discourse. New Zealand bureaucrats, academics and politicians have predominantly (but not solely) instigated this, citing a common currency and stock exchange, a strengthening of CER, greater bureaucratic harmony, and closer defence ties as desired outcomes. Indeed, former New Zealand prime minister Jim Bolger echoed these sentiments at the April 2000 constitutional conference when he said, 'If the Europeans can do that coming from their history, what does that suggest for two countries like New Zealand and Australia—two countries that because of so many points of shared history are closer than most? It raises the question of what new areas of cooperation, including shared institutions, we should now be exploring with our Australian neighbours.'[2]

It is the intention of this chapter to consider the state of the trans-Tasman relationship. Given the unique antipodean phenomenology of this chapter, the quandary of an appropriate paradigm to construct this inquiry will be addressed through three theoretical constructs. In the first instance, the evolving discourse of civic nationalism will be employed to highlight the inevitable divergence of independent and sovereign nation-states in both domestic and foreign policy where political elites are empowered to determine the 'national interest'. Secondly, having highlighted the basis for divergence between the antipodean nation-states, the Francis Fukyama argument, articulated in his germinal work *The End of History and the Last Man*, will be employed to illustrate how the ascendancy of the values of freedom, democracy and a market economy within both Australia and New Zealand has ensured that whenever these values have been challenged, both historically and currently, both nation-states have responded decisively (and often together) and are likely to continue to do so, despite differences of approach that may arise (from the first construct of divergent 'national interests'). Finally, the future of the trans-Tasman neighbours will be explored within the context of the future of nation-states in general, by surveying the phenomenon of economic convergence leading to the ontological fatalism for nation-states inherent in Gellner's constructivism.

Based on these considerations this chapter contends that the general state of the trans-Tasman relationship is positive—despite inevitable policy differences and irritants. Additionally, that the overarching commitment to liberal democratic and free-market values ensures an on-going and close defence and foreign policy relationship when participating on the international stage. And finally, that the antipodean nation-states are likely to experience greater economic harmonisation (although without political union in the short term).

Nationalism as a discourse

The discourse of nationalism has traditionally been built on two distinctive bases, broadly classified as primordialist and constructivist. Primordialists link the concept of the nation to its earliest incarnations, recognising its roots in ancient civilisations and societies.[3] From this perspective the concept of the nation featured in premodern Europe (and elsewhere) as monarchs and parliaments in European nations both claimed their legitimacy from their respective nations and served, at least in theory, to defend and protect the interests of these nations. As such, conceptually at least, the nation existed long before the nationalistic revolutions that mark the transition to modernity. By extension, the modern nation-states were drawn from these earlier incarnations of the nation. Smith, in reinforcing the primordialist perspective, describes nation-states as a historical consequence of ethnicity, culture and language, that attempts to translate the latent impetus of ethnic nations into political nation-states. National identities are therefore derived from the myths, legends, language and cultural histories of a particular historical context.[4]

Alternatively, constructivists contend that modern nation-states are a product of external forces, artificially moulding collective societies into a false sense of identity created for them. Gellner maintains that the demands of industrialisation have had direct implications for the existence of nation-states, indirectly creating new national cultures and by extension new national identities. Congruent with the development of an economic infrastructure, the necessity of providing basic levels of education harmonious with industrialisation fell to the nation-state. So too did the regulation of the market economies, which accommodated the benefit of manoeuvering these activities for national advantage. The obvious social consequences manifest in the side effects of industrialisation, particularly urbanisation—the relocation of significant portions of the population to large cities in search of work, and the detachment from the traditional sources of identity, the village and trade—allowed a sense of national identity to be imposed from above.[5] This was no more evident than in relation to language, a fundamental tenet of identity, where newly formed nation-states replaced the many dialects, or even different languages, of the various social groups of their citizens with state-sanctioned languages. This experience was compounded further as the European nation-states began expanding their borders through colonisation, thereby imposing these newly formed identities onto the indigenous peoples and settlers of these new territories.

Anderson offers an alternate constructivist perspective with some resonance and influence. The central tenet of his thesis is that modern nation-states are 'imagined political communities—and imagined as both inherently limited and sovereign'.[6] Unlike Gellner, Anderson does not accept that nationalism is a deliberate fabrication for economic ends, but instead posits that a misremembering and romanticising of the past, juxtaposed with a dramatic technological advancement both in the means of production but also more fundamentally in communications through print, has resulted in the forging of modern nation-states as imagined communities.[7]

The challenge for nationalism

What these discourses share is the legitimisation of the nation-state as the primary political unit within society, however this legitimacy is derived. However, the status of nations and nation-states occurs against a backdrop of competing ontological perspectives. Clearly, the unfolding discourse of nationalism has particular relevance for the questions in this chapter. However, no longer are the assumptions of the nation-state as the pre-eminent political unit totally valid. Congruent with this is the emerging reality that the long-standing debate between primordialists and constructivists has taken on new meanings as each becomes linked to a reinterpretation of multicultural societies within liberal democracies. Conceptually the antipodean nation-states are confronted with the reality of sovereignty being transferred to multinational and global political groupings, corporate entities far larger than themselves, and several subnational claims by indigenous groups, ethnic minorities and other interest groups. The ontological and epistemological link between indigenous and migrant cultures and a distinctive primordialist conception of legitimacy, is juxtaposed with the competing, and seemingly dominant, constructivist postcolonial antipodean nation-state derived from the enduring legacy of British colonial history. The outcome is a strained relationship between competing cultures for legitimacy, each displaying idiosyncratic world views and valuing disparate knowledge and learning accordingly. In making this assertion, the temptation to oversimplify the ontological and epistemological divergence in what are multicultural antipodean nation-states, by nominating the ethnic demographics in both and linking these to particular cultural characteristics, fails to accommodate the existential reality of individual identities forged in the social cleavages of both polities. However, as the scope of this chapter is limited both in size and subject matter, this concurrence of individual versus collective identities, while important to note, must be explored elsewhere.

Civic nationalism and the modern nation-state

The development of civic nationalism as an extension of the constructivist discourse offers a paradigm within which the strains of primordialist and constructivist claims to legitimacy can be reconciled (at least conceptually), while highlighting an aspect of divergence in the trans-Tasman relationship.

Civic nationalism, as articulated by the Canadian thinker Michael Ignatieff, is based on the pluralist ideal of 'a community of equal, rights bearing citizens united in a patriotic attachment to a shared set of political practices and values'.[8] Ignatieff contrasts this with 'ethnic nationalism' in which 'it is the national community which defines the individual, not the individuals who define the national community'.[9]

While Ignatieff's work is focused on his own personal crusade through post-Cold War Europe and his native Canada, the tenets of civic nationalism which he articulates provide a useful conceptual tool when applied to antipodean nation-states.

Ignatieff maintains that the basis of a civic nation is one of active pluralism in which the rights of citizenship are not dependent on ethnicity, religion, gender or language. The civic nation does display a communitarian quality, but it is one where the entire citizen base is equal before the law and generally embraces the key political and civil institutions. A fundamental element of the civic nation is the active democratic participation of its citizen base, through which the sovereignty of all citizens is reflected in institutions such as parliament.[10]

British sociologist John Hutchinson expands the foundation of the civic nation as one that includes a cosmopolitan and rationalist basis, in which the citizen base aspires to a 'common humanity which transcends cultural difference', but which accepts the role of democracy as the mechanism for achieving this ideal.[11] Habermas offers a model of a pluralist state that links the liberal principles of constitutional government, civil freedoms, and the rule of law, within a wider process of cultural innovation. In drawing upon the Aristotelian tradition of deliberative democracy, Habermas maintains an expression of consensus in which all participants have a vested interest in the possibility that all affected persons can engage in rational discourse. However, Habermas prefaces this view with the assertion that the interests of each person must be given equal consideration.[12]

Adjudicating over this pluralist sovereign entity are political elites who are empowered through these political systems with the ability to determine the 'national interest'. With a complicit citizen base, generally tolerant of other actors within the polity, and accepting of the role of elites in determining policy directions, political elites are free to pursue policy agendas in accordance with the constraints of the political system. Accountability within the system is provided through regular elections, with political elites forced to account for their performance and market themselves according to the effectiveness and saliency of their policy programme. The symbiotic nature of the relationship between political elites and their constituency ensures that their determination of the 'national interest' is generally a mix of the demands (and prejudices) of their constituency, and their own effectiveness in leading public discourse.

According to almost any measure that could be applied to defining a 'civic nation' (as outlined above) both Australia and New Zealand would comfortably fit. However, in illustrating the conformity of both nation-states as 'civic nations', an evident divergence in 'national interests' is also apparent. It is not the intention of this chapter to explore this in great detail, but rather to use two policy fronts—social policy and foreign affairs, trade and defence policy—to highlight two crucial elements of divergence of antipodean 'national interests', namely, their interpretation of pluralism and their sense of external threat.

Pluralism's two Antipodean faces: Biculturalism and multiculturalism
At face value the clear disparity between the percentage of the indigenous populations of Australia and New Zealand in relation to other population groups would provide the rationale for biculturalism in New Zealand and multiculturalism in Australia. With Maori representing 15 per cent of the New Zealand population (clearly the second largest ethnic population group) and Australia's Aboriginal population around 2 per cent (with several larger ethnic population groups) of its total, the relative level of political

influence each group potentially wields within a democratic system seems self-evident. This disparity is seemingly compounded by New Zealand's electoral system, the Mixed Member Proportional (MMP) system, which is based on proportional representation. Australia's lower house (the House of Representatives), which determines who governs, is elected using a preferential voting system which favours the larger parties and not minority interests (this is redressed somewhat through the Senate which uses a single transferable vote form of proportional representation and has seen minority interest groups such as the Greens elected). However, such demographic analysis does not address the true nature of biculturalism in New Zealand or multiculturalism in Australia.

For New Zealand's political elites it is the Treaty of Waitangi (colloquially referred to as the nation's founding document), rather than any demographic reality, which buttresses its bicultural foundation.

The 1995 State Services Commission document *The Public Service and Treaty of Waitangi* outlined the basic principles, conventions and practices that underpin the practical implementation of biculturalism in New Zealand. While the document is somewhat dated, its basic tenets remain in place. It outlines the 'principles of the treaty' as they had been articulated by the courts. These 'principles' oblige the government to 'act in good faith' when dealing with its treaty partner, acknowledging that the Crown must be allowed to govern in accordance with constitutional conventions, while preserving those rights given to Maori in article two of the treaty. This is sometimes referred to as the 'paramount principle'.[13] The 'principles of the treaty' also oblige the government to 'make informed decisions' and to 'not impede redress'.[14] While these principles and the role of the treaty have been a point of political contestability, nonetheless they have some saliency with the current Labour-led government, and feature in the policy formation process in New Zealand.

For Australians multiculturalism is a matter of government policy rather than a simple descriptor. In May 2003 the government released its policy programme for multiculturalism in the document *Multicultural Australia: United in Diversity.* This was an updated version of the 1999 document *New Agenda for Multicultural Australia.* The new document acts as a blueprint for all government activity as it relates to multiculturalism.

The document notes: 'Australian multiculturalism is the philosophy, underlying government policy and programs, that recognises, accepts, respects and celebrates Australia's cultural diversity. It embraces the heritage of Indigenous

Australians, early European settlement, our Australian-grown customs and those of the diverse range of migrants now coming to this country.'[15]

However it warns, 'the freedom of all Australians to express and share their cultural values is dependent on their abiding by mutual civic obligations. All Australians are expected to have an overriding loyalty to Australia and its people, and to respect the basic structures and principles underwriting our democratic society. These are the Constitution, Parliamentary democracy, freedom of speech and religion, English as the national language, the rule of law, acceptance and equality.'

One of the ultimate tests for any government is how it translates rhetoric into political reality. The test therefore for the governments of Australia and New Zealand, in their commitment to multiculturalism and biculturalism respectively, is how it is reflected in other policy. The impact of these two constructs on social policy highlights a divergence between Australia and New Zealand for two reasons. Firstly, because it clearly illustrates the unique approach to the principles of pluralism in both countries, based on historical and demographic circumstances. In New Zealand an explicit message of positive discrimination (based on the Treaty of Waitangi) is evident among its social services, while the delivery of Australia's social services is focused on the removal of any form of discrimination within a multicultural environment. Secondly, the provision of social services—primarily health, education and social welfare—is the largest component of government spending in both nation-states and highlights a key determinant of the 'national interest' in the allocation of each government's limited resources, accepting of course, that Australia is a federal system within which the administration of both health and education is devolved to the state governments (while the federal government remains the primary funder).

In New Zealand the current Labour-led government has stipulated six primary goals to provide the overarching direction for all policy development. One of these six is the goal to 'strengthen national identity and uphold the principles of the Treaty of Waitangi'.[16] A second goal is to 'reduce inequalities in health, education, employment and housing'.[17] The Ministry of Health, in adopting these goals, has explicitly undertaken an approach based on positive discrimination. Indeed, in its 2002 *Statement of Intent*, the ministry highlights that its highest priority is to 'concentrate on working to improve the health of Maori, Pacific peoples and those with fewest resources'.[18] The ministry is also focused on implementing *He Korowai Oranga* (the Maori Health Strategy) among its seven service priorities.[19]

Interestingly, the New Zealand Ministry of Education *Statement of Intent* begins its outcome focus section with the statement 'our focus is on better learning for every New Zealander'.[20] The ministry's assessment of where it needs to develop highlights the need for 'strong understanding of the aspirations and needs of Maori',[21] without emphasising any other ethnic or socio-economic cleavage. While the ministry acknowledges the growing diversity of New Zealand's population,[22] that is, only Maori are singled out for a special partnership aimed at reducing Maori underachievement and 'giving effect to the collaborative relationships envisaged in the Treaty of Waitangi'.[23] Like health, the Ministry of Education has also engaged specific 'population based strategies' aimed at Maori and Pacific populations.

The Ministry of Social Development (MSD) also pursues a programme of positive discrimination based on the Treaty of Waitangi. Indeed, among the specific 'client groups' identified by MSD only Maori are identified according to their ethnicity (with the others identified by age).[24] The Ministry notes in its *Statement of Intent* that 'as an agent of the Crown it acknowledges the Treaty of Waitangi as the founding document of New Zealand', adding the need to be responsive to the treaty by 'ensuring that Maori interests are protected and are given appropriate priority in all aspects of the work the Ministry undertakes'.[25] However, the ministry makes the observation that 'even if the treaty did not exist, it would be just as important to consider the needs of Maori, and to use everything at our disposal to achieve acceptable outcomes for Maori'.[26]

The focus by social agencies in New Zealand on Maori and Pacific Island populations can be justified as more than simple obligations under the Treaty of Waitangi (in the case of Maori). As the MSD *Statement of Intent* highlights 'in the last twenty years life expectancy for all New Zealanders has increased, but Maori and Pacific peoples still have a considerably shorter life expectancy than other groups. While the health outcomes of Maori and Pacific peoples are improving, comparisons with New Zealand averages show there is a lot of room for improvement.'[27]

The Australian Department of Health and Ageing invokes a different approach to the pluralist principle. In its *Corporate Plan*, the department highlights 'equitable access' and 'fostering a healthier community' among its overarching objectives.[28] However, a perusal of the department's *Corporate Plan* and other related material highlights that the only form of positive discrimination that is evident is in relation to the treatment of the aged, with no reference to specific ethnicities.

The Australian Department of Education, Science and Training does specify among its 'key results areas' within its *Corporate Plan* the aim to 'improve participation, accessibility and learning outcomes for Indigenous Australians'.[29] The department adds that among its 'business priorities' is the desire to 'redress the significant gaps between the educational outcomes of Indigenous and non-Indigenous Australians'.[30]

The Australian Department of Family and Community Services (FaCS) Strategic Statement 2002–05 maintains its overarching vision is to achieve 'a fair and cohesive Australian society'.[31] However, like the Commonwealth Department of Health and Ageing, no specific mention of either indigenous or other ethnic populations is evident among the department's high-level policy statements.

It must be made clear that the intent of this chapter is not to assert that one approach to social service policy development and delivery is better than the other, or that one is 'right' and the other 'wrong', but rather to highlight that they are different, divergent, and a consequence of political elites determining the 'national interest' in each nation-state. The key to this exercise is to understand the primacy of the Treaty of Waitangi for political elites in social policy formation and delivery in New Zealand when compared to Australia. Indeed, the only reference to indigenous Australians in the high-level policy formation and delivery statements of the three social agencies considered was the reference to the need to reduce disparities in educational performance. Ironically, among the same agencies in New Zealand, only MSD noted that it would apply the same level of attention to Maori needs 'even if the treaty did not exist'. This highlights the fundamental divergence between the bicultural foundation which confronts New Zealand political elites, compared to the implicit multicultural basis of Australian society.

Same bed, different nightmares[32]

The statement above is borrowed from comments made by Hugh White, a former Australian Deputy Secretary of Defence and currently the Director of the Australian Strategic Policy Institute, to the 36th Otago Foreign Policy School in 2001. White was responding to questions on the nature of the perceived threats to the trans-Tasman neighbours as it affected their defence and foreign policies. White added that what he meant by the statement was that in his view Australia's sense of threat was related to the possibility of military or other threats to its territory and was less focused on a sense of economic vulnerability. New Zealand on the other hand, was far more concerned over its exposure economically and far less concerned about the need to militarily defend its territory. One need only peruse local New Zealand media coverage of the negotiations between Australia and the US for a free-trade agreement to discern the sense of paranoia that New Zealand may miss out to see that White's thesis has some merit.

White began his paper to the Foreign Policy School with the words 'at last its official. Australia and New Zealand are going separate ways on Strategic policy'.[33] White was commenting on the New Zealand Labour-led government's decision to abandon much of its navy and air strike capability, while Australia was embarking on a policy to increase its long-term defence spending. White added that this shift in focus represented a fundamental turning point of the magnitude for New Zealand's nuclear free policy.[34] He claimed that the New Zealand government's decisions marked the end of the 'single strategic entity' concept between both countries and would strain the 'Closer Defence Relationship' (CDR) forged in the post-nuclear policy environment. Allan Behm, Director of the Canberra-based Knowledge Pond, told a conference on trans-Tasman relations in 2002, in unequivocal terms, that 'at the level of both theoretical and technical sophistication, the armed forces of both Australia and New Zealand are diverging'.[35]

New Zealand's strategic policy was clearly articulated within its 2000 *Defence Policy Framework* which unequivocally claims that New Zealand's strategic policy will be based on its own assessment of external threats.[36] These include: defending New Zealand, including its people, lands and territorial waters to the Exclusive Economic Zone; assisting in the maintenance of security in the South Pacific and providing assistance to Pacific neighbours; meeting New Zealand's alliance commitments to Australia through close partnerships in pursuit of common security interests; playing an appropriate role in the Asia-Pacific region; and contributing to global security and peacekeeping through participation in the full range of UN and other appropriate multilateral peace support and relief operations.[37]

This view was further reinforced by Prime Minister Clark in a media interview in which she stated: 'We're not a single strategic entity . . . the New Zealand interest is also close cooperation with Australia, but first we stand back and say what is the New Zealand interest.'[38]

Indeed, the Labour-led government, in formally announcing the reorientation of New Zealand's defence forces in May 2000, stated that based on advice from the External Assessments Bureau and the Ministry of

Foreign Affairs and Trade New Zealand confronted 'an incredibly benign strategic reality'. Clark has defended this assessment several times since making the announcement, including in the aftermath of the 11 September 2001 terrorist attacks and the more recent Bali bombings on 12 October 2002. She told parliament on 15 October 2002 that 'that statement was made in relation to direct threats from any other country, and still applies in that sense'.[39] However, Clark added that the government would 'continue to do everything in its power to protect New Zealanders from such threats and to contribute to international counter-terrorism'.[40]

In its 2003 annual report the New Zealand Ministry of Foreign Affairs and Trade noted that 'the international environment in which New Zealand pursues its external objectives remains complex and unpredictable'.[41] It noted that the ministry was strengthening its policy focus on counter terrorism, and was committed to on-going participation in 'Operation Enduring Freedom' and the establishment of a Pacific Regional Security Fund.[42]

Australia's strategic focus is enunciated in its 2002 Foreign Affairs and Trade Policy White Paper *Advancing the National Interest*. This document says that Australia will seek to build on its relationships in trade and investment with Asia, the United States (US), Western Europe, New Zealand and the Middle East; on its defence relationship with the US and important intelligence partners; and on strong people-to-people links with the Asia-Pacific, US, Canada, Europe and the United Kingdom (UK).[43] The relationship Australia has with the United States was described as 'fundamental for our security and prosperity'[44] and is unequivocally Australia's most importance alliance.

Australia's strategic policy was acknowledged in the 2003 release of *Australia's National Security: A Defence Update 2003*. This document noted that in the two years since the Department of Defence had released its White Paper in 2000 'we are in no doubt the strategic landscape has changed'.[45] The document notes that 'the strategic environment is being shaped by the threat of terrorism and the determination to counter it'.[46] The prospect of a direct military threat to Australian territory was diminished due to the strong Australia–US alliance and US primacy. However, the unstable nature of the South-East Asia region and the South Pacific would place increased demands on Australia in the region.[47]

While the above is an abridged version of what is a complex and vast policy front, it does, however, serve as an indicative account of the policy divergence of the antipodean nation-states. Again it must be stressed that the intent of this chapter is not to assert that the foreign affairs and defence policies of either nation-state is 'better', 'right' or 'wrong'. That is for the citizen base of both to decide. The key point is that they are different, significantly so, and are a feature of the relationship. There are several evident points of disjuncture between both nation-states:

- New Zealand's overarching commitment to multilateralism compared to the pre-eminence of the US alliance to Australia (Australia remains an active member of the ANZUS treaty while New Zealand does not)
- New Zealand's niche role in providing peacekeeping forces compared to Australia's commitment to ensuring that its strike force capability is maintained
- Australia's far broader sense of threat from other nation-states as well as terrorist and other non-state actors compared to New Zealand's assessment of a 'benign strategic reality'
- Australia's greater fiscal commitment to defence (almost 2 per cent of gross domestic product) compared to New Zealand (around 1 per cent).

Interestingly, with the Howard government's recent reorientation of Australia's foreign policy placing greater emphasis on its role in the Pacific, what had previously been a point of divergence, is potentially a point of confluence.

The end of history for the Antipodean nation-states

One of the more influential contributions to the meta-narrative of modernity in recent years has been Francis Fukuyama's germinal work *The End of History and the Last Man*. The central thesis in Fukuyama's work is his contention that the contest of ideas and ideology which is a central feature of modernity is essentially over. He claims that history is directional and points toward the ascendancy of market economies and liberal democracies over other ideological narratives (in particular Marxist socialism). Fukuyama uses Hegelian dialectics (the contest between theses and antitheses creating new syntheses which become new theses) to trace the ideological struggles of modernity, citing the fall of Eastern European communism and the rapid market liberalisation of China as a sign of his own thesis coming to fruition.[48]

While Fukuyama has had his critics, many of whom have grown more vocal in the post September 11 climate, (with some pointing to Samuel Huntington's *Clash of Civilizations and the Remaking of World Order* as a more accurate account of the state of modernity) his central thesis holds true for the antipodean nation-states.

The contest of ideas within both countries (in particular among the major political parties) occurs at the margins and is generally evident through incremental policy shifts towards a degree of emphasis rather than complete paradigm change. The pre-eminence of liberal democratic values, the rule of law, and the market economy, is well established.

Both nation-states also have a long tradition of fighting for these values (both metaphorically and literally) wherever they are threatened. Not only did Australia and New Zealand actively participate in the great wars of modernity, forging close links within the Australian and New Zealand Army Corps (ANZAC) tradition, as the new threat of terrorism encroached on both nation-states, each responded decisively in international terms to combat this growing scourge.

While critics on either side of the Tasman may point to the participation or non-participation in the US-led war in Iraq as a signal of the growing divergence between both nation-states, this assessment loses sight of the overarching picture. Both are actively engaged in the war on terror. Both have troops deployed overseas in the cause and both have enacted domestic legislation consistent with UN resolutions in the fight against terrorism. Both have engaged in regional efforts to limit the extent terrorism can take root in the region and both have responded to regional concerns such as East Timor, Bougainville and the Solomon Islands. There will always be divergence about the means of achieving any particular end while two groups of elites are empowered to make such decisions, but it is no coincidence that both nation-states are aligned in international efforts where their shared values are under threat.

Two nations: One nation: No nation-state
An interesting consequence of the expansion of the European Union has been the reinvigoration of convergence theories driven by economic rationales. One account of this perspective is found in the ontological fatalism with regard to nation-states inherent in Gellner's constructivism. On the one hand Gellner asserts that industrial societies will ultimately dissolve the diversity of culture and organisation that are a feature of the modern nation-state, replacing it instead with a globally homogenised culture and organisation

congruent with economic and technological demands. Alternatively, Gellner maintains that as ethnic groups, within existing nation-states, assert their claims to sovereignty, then inevitably violent uprisings and disruption of conventional models of nation-states will occur. Gellner cites post-Cold War European, Balkan, African, South American and Asian examples to support his thesis.[49]

Gellner is not alone in these assertions. The consequential implications for nation-states of an encroaching global economy is addressed by Berger who suggests that the prospect of advancing technology accessible to all, the growing implementation of 'best practice' methods in industry, and enforced conformity to fiscal and economic policy by international groups, such as the International Monetary Fund (IMF), the World Trade Organisation(WTO), the European Union (EU), the Asia-Pacific Economic Cooperation (APEC) movement and the North American Free Trade Agreement (NAFTA), will inevitably lead to convergence in the global economy, making nation-states redundant.[50] Boyer adds that convergence theories have come to include not only economic performance, but also the basis of interaction between the polity and the economy.[51]

The convergence of the antipodean economies was set firmly in track with the signing of the Closer Economic Relations (CER) agreement in 1983. This process had begun in embryonic form in 1965 with the New Zealand Australia Free Trade Agreement. By the late 1970s it had resulted in the removal of tariffs and quantitative restrictions on around 80 per cent of trans-Tasman trade. However, the lack of a formal mechanism to further advance the progress made under the New Zealand Australia Free Trade Agreement was recognised by political elites on both sides of the Tasman, and the ground work for CER was put in place from 1980 onwards.[52]

Indeed, the inertia CER created was enhanced in three general reviews in 1988, 1992 and 1995. With each review came a greater commitment to harmonisation. The 1988 review led to the 'Protocol on Acceleration of Free Trade in Goods' which, since July 1990, has ensured that all goods meeting the CER rules of origin have been free of tariffs, tariff quotas and quantitative import restrictions. A second element of the 1988 review was the 'Protocol on Harmonisation of Quarantine Procedures' which has improved the speed and efficiency of the flow of goods between both nation-states. A third aspect of the review was the crucial inclusion of services into the agreement with the 'Protocol on Trade in Services'. This move has ensured that all services within both nation-states, beyond those specified, are considered the same by both governments. The review has also resulted in progress being made on government purchasing, the harmonisation of customs policies, business law coordination, industry assistance and the reduction of technical barriers to trade.[53]

The 1992 review ensured the harmonisation process continued with both nation-states considering the merits of New Zealand joining Australia in mutual recognition schemes for product stands and various register occupations. The review also refined the rules of origin process and updated the list of services exempted in the 'Protocol on Trade in Services'. A further outcome was the agreement to institute annual trade and economic officials' talks in conjunction with the trade ministers' annual talks.

The 1995 review focused on eliminating the remaining regulatory barriers to trade, colloquially labelled 'third generation' issues. The 'Protocol on Trade in Services' was further developed with Australia making significant concessions on postal services and telecommunications, and New Zealand on aviation and shipping. The rules of origin process was also revisited. It was also decided that all subsequent reviews of CER would occur annually and would feature as part of the trade ministers' annual meetings.[54]

The process of harmonisation has not slowed. On-going incremental progress has occurred across a number of fronts. In 1996 the 'Trans-Tasman Mutual Recognition Arrangement' (TTMRA) was signed, as was the 'Agreement on Joint Food Standards' which established the Australia New Zealand Food Authority (ANZFA). In 1997 New Zealand became a full member of the 'Australian Government Procurement Agreement'. In 2002 the 'Open Skies Agreement' was signed, effectively creating a single aviation market, and the 'Agreement on Joint Food Standards' was amended, with ANZFA renamed Food Standards Australia New Zealand (FSANZ).[55] Further progress occurred in 2003 on a proposed trans-Tasman Therapeutic Goods Agency and with the announcement of annual meetings for finance ministers to join the prime ministers, foreign ministers, trade ministers and defence ministers who meet at least annually (along with the many other ministers who meet intermittently on Australia's Ministerial Councils).

In a thoughtful analysis of the prospects for the trans-Tasman market the New Zealand Institute of Economic Research (NZIER) produced a working paper *Stepping Towards a Borderless Market? The Future of the Trans-Tasman Market*. The NZIER suggested several issues needed addressing for a truly borderless market to occur including: revisiting rules of origin within a globalising context; harmonising the tax systems; broadening the harmonisation of regulations; greater consistency within the immigration policies and airline rules; and some form of congruency in the bodies that govern competition laws.[56]

The counterbalance to this process of economic integration is the limiting effect of political constraints. Any move toward greater harmonisation generates tensions. It principally requires resolving the quandary that exists when articulating the rationale for an economic union, particularly in the context of growing regional and global economies, and within the increasingly complex context of culture and identity. The juxtaposition of the economic rationale for union, and cultural claims to remain separate, is set in a global political environment in flux. As Hobsbawm reminds us in his reflections on world society's move to a new millennium, never in our collective histories has humanity shared so much knowledge about, or moved so freely among, each other, and in essence experienced a truly global community.[57]

However, the stepping stones of progress toward regional and truly global unions are slow and arduous. What seems clear in the trans-Tasman relationship is that despite the political will (generally echoed in the business community) and impetus for greater economic harmonisation, there is little appetite on either side of the Tasman for full political union. Not only would this proposition face several significant constitutional hurdles, the lack of a popular will among the wider populations of both nation-states would limit any prospects of unification.

Conclusion

The intent of this chapter was to illustrate that as civic nations displaying a form of civic nationalism, in which political elites determine the 'national interest', divergence inevitably occurs. While only two policy fronts—social policy and foreign affairs and defence policy—were used to illustrate this point, any of a myriad of overlapping policies within the policy nexus of both nation-states could have been employed. However, the choice of policy fronts unmistakably highlighted several key points of difference and divergence in these trans-Tasman neighbour's sense of 'national interest'.

With pluralism reflected in policy formation through biculturalism in New Zealand and multiculturalism in Australia, a fundamental divide in the delivery of social policy is clearly evident between the antipodean nation-states. A visibly divergent view of strategic realities is also evident in foreign affairs and defence policy, and like social policy this is translated into divergent policy delivery.

However, despite this influence of divergence, an overarching commitment to the values of a liberal democracy, the rule of law and a market economy has ensured that whenever these values have been threatened the antipodean nation-states have resolutely acted to promote and preserve them. Both nations have also forged such close economic ties that the dilemma of how to further harmonise the two economies has become particularly pertinent.

The antipodean nation-states cannot escape their geography or their historical links. With divergent 'national interests' openly acknowledged it seems apparent that the antipodean neighbours face one of two choices. Either they can acknowledge that differences exist and move ahead constructively together accepting the limitations of these divergent views. Alternatively, dissonance on both sides can be allowed to fester, hindering the relationship and ensuring that it is built on a negative footing. Clearly while in some quarters there remains a determination to pursue the latter path, on the evidence of the past few years political elites on both sides of the Tasman have chosen the former.

The professional and constructive relationship that the present governments of Australia and New Zealand display in acknowledging divergence without allowing it to hinder progress, provides a sound basis for the on-going relationship. The past several years has seen the removal of the social security issue as an irritant; the resolution of the Tampa issue; joint and regional efforts in East Timor, the Solomon's and Bougainville; joint efforts in the WTO on people smuggling, counter terrorism and on numerous other fronts, all of which demonstrate the depth of political will on both sides for a constructive relationship. Given the above, arriving at a positive outlook for the future of the trans-Tasman relationship seems both feasible and justified.

It is widely accepted that Malcolm Fraser and Robert Muldoon seldom saw eye to eye and were a source of antagonism for each other. And yet CER was negotiated and signed under their watch. If this type of success was achieved under such negative circumstances, a salient question for the trans-Tasman relationship must be what could be achieved with two leaders well disposed to each other and with the political will for progress? Only time will tell.

Notes

1 While I was an employee of the Australian High Commission at the time I wrote, the views expressed in this chapter are my own and should not be attributed to the High Commission or the Australian Department of Foreign Affairs and Trade.
2 J. Bolger, 'The American Constitutional Experience and Issues of Sovereignty: Lessons for New Zealand' in C. James (ed), *Building the Constitution* (Wellington, Institute of Policy Studies, 2000), p.57.
3 D. Miller, *On Nationality* (Oxford, Claredin Press, 1995), p.28.
4 A. Smith, *National Identity* (London, Penguin, 1991).
5 E. Gellner, *Nationalism* (London, Phoenix, 1997), pp.25–30.
6 B. Anderson, *Imagined Communities: Reflections on the Origins and Spread of Nationalism*, revised edition (London, Verso, 1991), p.9.
7 Anderson, *Imagined Communities*, p.9.
8 M. Ignatieff, *Blood and Belonging: Journeys into the New Nationalism* (New York, Noonday Press, 1995), p.5.
9 Ignatieff, *Blood and Belonging*, p.5.
10 Ignatieff, *Blood and Belonging*, pp.5–9.
11 J. Hutchinson, *The Dynamics of Cultural Nationalism* (London, Allen and Unwin, 1987), pp.12–13.
12 J. Habermas, *Between Facts and Norms: Contributions to a Discourse Theory of Law and Democracy* (Oxford, Polity Press, 1996).
13 State Services Commission, *The Public Service and Treaty of Waitangi* (Wellington, State Services Commission, 1995), p.3.
14 State Services Commission, *The Public Service and Treaty of Waitangi*, p.3.
15 Commonwealth of Australia, *Multicultural Australia: United in Diversity* (Commonwealth of Australia, 2003), p.7.
16 State Services Commission, *Managing for Outcomes: Guidance for Government Departments* (Wellington, State Services Commission, 2003).
17 State Services Commission, *Managing for Outcomes*.
18 Ministry of Health, *Statement of Intent* (2002), p.12.
19 Ministry of Health, *Statement of Intent* (2002), p.11.
20 Ministry of Education, *Statement of Intent* (2003), p.5.
21 Ministry of Education, *Statement of Intent* (2003), p.8.
22 Ministry of Education, *Statement of Intent* (2003), p.8.
23 Ministry of Education, *Statement of Intent* (2003), p.10.
24 Ministry of Social Development, *Statement of Intent* (2003), p.5.
25 Ministry of Social Development, *Statement of Intent* (2003), p.20.
26 Ministry of Social Development, *Statement of Intent* (2003), p.20.
27 Ministry of Social Development, *Statement of Intent* (2003), p.12.
28 Department of Health and Ageing, *Corporate Plan: Better Health, Better Life, Better Care 2003–2005* (Commonwealth of Australia, 2003), p.5.
29 Department of Education, Science and Technology, *Corporate Plan* (Commonwealth of Australia, 2002), p.3.

30 Department of Education, Science and Technology, *Corporate Plan*, p.4.
31 Department of Family and Community Services, *Strategic Statement 2002–2005* (Commonwealth of Australia, 2002), p.2.
32 This phrase was used by Hugh White, the former Australian Deputy Secretary of Defence, in response to a question on the state of the trans-Tasman strategic relationship at the Otago Foreign Policy School in 2002.
33 H. White, 'Living Without Illusions: Where does our Defence Relationship Go From Here', in R. Catley (ed), *Moving Together or Drifting Apart* (Wellington, Dark Horse Publishing, 2002), p.129.
34 H. White, 'Living Without Illusions', p.129.
35 A. Behm, 'Defence and Security Across the Tasman' in A. Grimes, L. Wevers and G. Sullivan, *States of Mind: Australia and New Zealand* 1901–2001 (Wellington, Institute of Policy Studies, 2002), p.100.
36 New Zealand Defence Forces, *The Government's Defence Policy Framework* (Wellington, 2000), p.3.
37 New Zealand Defence Forces, *The Government's Defence Policy Framework*, pp.3–5.
38 R. Laugesen, 'Clark splits from Australians on military matters', *Sunday Star Times*, 27 February 2000, p.2 .
39 *Hansard*, Answers to Parliamentary Oral Questions, 15 October 2002.
40 *Hansard*, Answers to Parliamentary Oral Questions, 15 October 2002.
41 Ministry of Foreign Affairs and Trade, *Annual Report* (Wellington, Ministry of Foreign Affairs and Trade, 2003), p.4 .
42 Ministry of Foreign Affairs and Trade, *Annual Report*, p.5.
43 Department of Foreign Affairs and Trade, *Advancing the National Interest* (Canberra, National Capital Printing, 2002), p.10.
44 Department of Foreign Affairs and Trade, *Advancing the National Interest*, p.4.
45 Department of Defence, *Australia's National Security: A Defence Update 2003* (Commonwealth of Australia, 2003), p.7.
46 Department of Defence, *Australia's National Security*, p.23.
47 Department of Defence, *Australia's National Security*, p.23.
48 Francis Fukuyama, *The End of History and the Last Man* (New York, Avon, 1993).
49 E. Gellner, *Nationalism* (London, Phoenix, 1997).
50 S. Berger, 'Introduction' in S. Berger and R. Dore (eds), *National Diversity and Global Capitalism* (New York, Cornell University Press, 1996).
51 R. Boyer, 'The Convergence Hypothesis Revisited' in S. Berger and R. Dore (ed), *National Diversity and Global Capitalism* (New York, Cornell University Press, 1996).
52 *Report of the Foreign Affairs, Defence and Trade Select Committee: Inquiry into New Zealand's Economic and Trade Relationship with Australia* (Wellington, House of Representatives, 2002).
53 *Report of the Foreign Affairs, Defence and Trade Select Committee*, 2002.
54 *Report of the Foreign Affairs, Defence and Trade Select Committee*, 2002.
55 *Report of the Foreign Affairs, Defence and Trade Select Committee*, 2002.
56 New Zealand Institute of Economic Research, *Stepping Towards a Borderless Market? The Future of the Trans-Tasman Market* (Wellington, NZIER, 2003), p.24.
57 E. Hobsbawm, *On the Edge of the New Century* (London, New Press, 2001), p.117.

14

IT'S THE REGION, STUPID!

Denis McClean

It is interesting and may be instructive that trans-Tasman relations are a constant theme for academic discussions on foreign policy in New Zealand. In Australia the subject seems not to come up. The Oxford Companion to New Zealand Literature devotes a longish section to trans-Tasman literature, that is, to writings and writers representative of a sense of a shared Australian-New Zealand outlook. The Oxford Companion to Australian Literature, published in 1991, finds no space at all for comment on the interactions between Australian and New Zealand literature. In New Zealand closer economic relations (CER) are constantly trotted out as an index of the value and pertinence of the Australia-New Zealand economic connection. Yet, in a very random sample, three recent studies of the Australian economy during the 1980s and early 1990s make no mention of CER at all.

We need to think why this is so. Why are issues to do with New Zealand a matter of indifference in Australia?

Major cricket tours of England used to begin with a match against a side selected by the Duke of Norfolk with the Duke himself as captain. In a match against the Australians, the Duke's butler once had to be pressed into service as an umpire. Sure enough the poor man was faced with a terrible dilemma. The Duke took a wild swipe at the ball which hit him firmly on the pad straight in front of his wicket. He was plainly out. The Australians appealed very loudly and aggressively and all eyes turned on the hapless butler. His boss glared at him from the opposite crease. What was he to say? Finally he remembered the words he used every day. 'His Grace,' he said, 'is not in.'

On this side of the Tasman we seem to have a similar capacity for trying not to face the reality of our dealings with Australia. Like the Duke's butler we simply don't seem to be able to decide whether we want to be in or out, partners or not, allies or only occasional associates. The relationship with the country which is indisputably more important to us than any other is bedevilled by myths about the Australia New Zealand Army Corps (ANZAC) and all that and by more opportunism and spin than any Australian bowler could ever serve up to the Duke of Norfolk. It is time to move on—to face the facts.

We should start by looking at the map. New Zealanders tend to think that the term Austral-asia is used by Australians only when they want to claim some New Zealander or some New Zealand success as one of their own—without actually mentioning the word New Zealand. For that sort of reason New Zealanders tend to dislike the term. But of course in a strategic sense, Austral-asia describes what we are. Austral-asia brings together Australia, New Zealand, New Guinea and the islands of Oceania. This is where we live.

To put it bluntly the basic challenge faced by Australia and New Zealand is how to deal with the fact of being Western nations—by history, by political instincts, and in terms of our relative economic performance—situated a long way away from our fellow members of this group. We sit to the south of Asia. We are Austral-asians. We share a distinct, extended and difficult strategic area. We face what look like escalating problems in coping with the region in which we must make our way.

Yet over a hundred years ago New Zealand declared its independence—not from Britain but from Australia. In determining not to join the Australian Commonwealth New Zealand turned away from the development of a concerted approach to the region in which it lives. It was the most important foreign policy choice we have ever made, and it was made almost in a fit of absence of mind. It has shaped our world view ever since. In 1901 New Zealand 'passed' on the need to define relations with Australia in immediate and vital terms representative of the regional realities. Instead we sought a surrogate on the other side of the world which would not threaten our own rather fragile sense of national identity. We have continued to look for such alternatives.

For well over half a century the British Empire provided a more than adequate stage for us to parade our ambitions and views of the world. The Empire—all-embracing, all-powerful—provided for both countries, but more so for New Zealand, a substitute for regional and strategic thought.

If our politicians could happily see themselves strutting the imperial stage in London what cause was there for New Zealanders to mix in with the Australians in their absurd little backwater in Canberra? When the

Empire provided the economic framework, what cause was there to think in terms of an integrated trans-Tasman economic community? If the Royal Navy was there to provide for imperial defence, why bother with the hard issues of working out defence arrangements best suited to our own region in association with Australia? Indeed, in New Zealand's case, why bother thinking about defence at all? That disposition, I might add, has stayed with us—long after the demise of the Empire which gave it at least partial justification.

The conduct of foreign relations within the Empire was famously described as 'everyone writing home to Mother; nobody writing to one another'. This was hub and spoke politics with a vengeance. As between Australia and New Zealand the outcome was a sad failure to come to grips with the strategic reality of their overlapping and shared, indeed, intertwined destinies.

The only serious attempt to move in the opposite direction was an Australian initiative—the Canberra or ANZAC Pact of 1944. After being given the back of the hand by their great power allies during World War II, the two countries agreed to coordinate their regional interests with the aim of securing their position in the Pacific. As is well known, London and Washington were affronted by the presumption of this scheme. The framework for trans-Tasman collaboration which it established proved overambitious. The two countries soon found that they had other fish to fry and the ANZAC Pact—although it still serves as a model—met the fate reserved for overenthusiastic and overly zealous diplomatic enterprises.

After the war there was a revolution in international affairs. The progressive collapse of the European and American empires produced an avalanche of new sovereignties. The United Nations provided a new focus for hopes of multilateralism. But paradoxically the United Nations Charter set in concrete concepts of national sovereignty and independence which defined a new international order in which nationalism could bloom as a dominating impulse.

So this is the first point I would like to make. The strange and strained relationship between Australia and New Zealand is a product of a time when each country was thinking about something else. Before World War II republican sentiment in Australia, which might have fostered the idea of a greater Austral-asia, never stood a chance against the prevailing empire loyalty. By the same token regional thinking, with its notions of an ANZAC community of interest, was blotted out in New Zealand by an overwhelming sense of commitment to an imperial ideal. The empire stood for collective security, monetary union within the sterling area, and comfortable trading arrangements centred on the London market.

These things—and this is my second point—made it possible for the relationship between Australia and New Zealand to become snared in petty nationalism. A growing Australian sense of destiny left little room for an association with New Zealand. New Zealand had chosen not to join the great Australian cavalcade and thus by definition, and almost inevitably, lost significance in Australian eyes. A relationship of unequals was established. Australian disdain for little New Zealand would be matched only by a New Zealand determination not to be taken for granted by Australia. In Australian eyes New Zealand was doomed to be forever a lesser satellite revolving around the bright sun of the Australian Commonwealth. In the same fashion New Zealanders learned to stew in prejudices about Australia—too big for its boots; ideas above its station; always winning test matches in extra time, and so on. The usual impedimenta of nationalism—to do with land and geography, language and literature, identity and national culture—was gradually added to the trans-Tasman mix. On both sides of the Tasman the nationalistic brew was made more potent by much intellectual posturing about the two countries as places apart, new and different worlds in the south—God's Own Countries.

It has all been less than convincing. It is obvious, as the Australian commentator Philip Adams has put it, that it would be impossible to find, anywhere, two countries more boringly similar. Australia and New Zealand, for all the petty nationalism, are simply more like each other than either is with any other country in the world. What is more, although the respective national interests of the two countries may not be identical, they are virtually inseparable.

When the Australians own the banks and the railways, when much of the New Zealand media is run from Australia, when the capital and share markets are hugely interactive, when travel between the two countries is routine and intensive, when about a tenth of the New Zealand population lives in Australia, what is the point in pretending that the interests of the two countries are not intertwined? When Australia is New Zealand's most important trading partner, it is hard to know where the pretence that New Zealand has great freedom of manoeuvre comes from. New Zealanders often proclaim that if ever Australia were attacked or otherwise in trouble, we would be there picking up the cudgels to help. By definition this means that we accept that our strategic interests overlap with those of Australia. Yet it is maintained in high places in Wellington that the two countries do not constitute a strategic entity. New Zealand, it is routinely and rather tediously proclaimed, is a country of the South Pacific while Australia looks to Asia. But when push came to shove New Zealand readily accepts that it has strong interests in East Timor, on Australia's Asian front, while Australia has recently shown itself persuaded of the importance of its own interests in the Pacific, our so-called area of interest, by intervening strongly in the Solomon Islands.

In a rapidly globalising world, compartmentalisation of New Zealand interests and Australian interests no longer makes sense. The two countries do constitute a strategic entity and must begin to orient policies in order to maximise their respective capacities to develop and prosper as the world changes around them.

There is a story of two preachers, one a Methodist and the other a Presbyterian, arguing about the respective advantages of their particular brands of the Christian faith. They go at it hammer and tongs for a long time. Finally the Methodist flies the flag of surrender: 'After all, we can agree on one thing, we both worship the same God.' 'Yes', replies the Presbyterian in triumph, 'you in your way and I in his.'

We must be able to do better than this. We need to look beyond such convictions about our own righteousness. There has to be a better course for Australia and New Zealand than to continue to insist—I do it my way. We must learn more effectively to develop Austral-asian attitudes.

The ANZAC Pact was pushed by Herbert Evatt, the vigorous and rather splendid Australian minister of external affairs, who could see the advantage of the two countries working together to stake out their interests in the Pacific. He believed that the two should be able to think alike and to work together to cope with the issues of the region. The great-power partners, the British and the Americans, objected strenuously to the idea that Australia and New Zealand should lay out their own interests in this way.

There has been no comparable burst of political enthusiasm for the idea of Austral-asian togetherness since that time, from either side of the Tasman. There is obviously between New Zealand and Australia none of the brutal differences over ideology, race, language, religion or tribalism which have fuelled so much nationalistic strife elsewhere. Even so, it seems that two countries with so much in common are being blind-sided by nationalism. If this is so, then we will have no foundation for building a truly effective, collaborative, interactive Austral-asia, no matter what governments are in power in the two countries.

A strategic partnership of the kind which needs to be built between Australia and New Zealand is not to be defined solely in military or defence terms. To my mind this is a civilisational issue that transcends military or security calculations. The arguments in favour of New Zealand and Australia making common cause are about two relatively small countries achieving economies of scale, becoming more effective through pooling of their resources, assets and talents, and integrating their military, educational and professional systems. In response to the demands of the modern knowledge-based global economy, close collaboration would permit construction of a broader and deeper research and development base. It might even be possible in the process to work together to iron out constitutional anomalies both have inherited from the British and thus to generate a new sense of momentum and commitment in both countries. A more diverse Austral-asian community would provide a broader foundation for the development of productive economic as well as political relationships with Asia and the Pacific. Removal of all impediments to trade and exchange would be capable of triggering new economic dynamism to match the potential of the region. A broader base to Antipodean society would offer more scope for the incorporation of our peoples of different origins and ethnic beliefs, as the history of the United States has demonstrated.

It is a given that the trans-Tasman skein of connections is already far-reaching and intensive, and is consolidated on a daily, almost hourly, basis by cross-investment and mutually interpenetrative business and commercial arrangements. Diplomatic interactions are relaxed and informal, and the politicians are now in regular and systematic contact. Consultation and coordination of efforts across a wide spectrum of government business has become almost instinctive.

But underlying it are a number of fundamental roadblocks to consolidation. These include the impact of a very rigid Australian Constitution, the absence of a basis for bringing together the two judicial systems in a concerted appeals structure and the absence of New Zealand experience of the intricacies of Federal-State politics, which puts a crimp on the ability to talk the same political language. It need hardly be mentioned that issues relating to alliance with the United States, and thus to do with the entire security context in Asia and the Pacific, are, to say the least, now being approached from different directions by the two countries. We can, in present circumstances, forget about New Zealand seeking political union with Australia. Such a fundamental renunciation of sovereignty on the part of New Zealand is inconceivable. What is more, the practical difficulties in bringing off such a profound change within the constraints of the Australian Constitution, not to speak of the need to accommodate the Treaty of Waitangi processes in New Zealand, seem insurmountable.

So which way do we turn to consolidate a deeper and more profound sense of regional partnership? I suggest there is something of a tussle in the minds of New Zealanders. On the one hand there are those who believe that because of our unique geographical location it is possible to espouse notions of singularity and separatism. This is not about disengagement—that option has never been espoused by New Zealand—rather it is to do with an ideal of sturdy independence, of cleaving to lonely courses which might afford moral satisfaction but tend to distance us from the interests of the countries with which we have most in common.

On the other hand there are those, and obviously I am one of them, who believe that a small country needs to work with its traditional partners, needs to be able to pool resources with them and to commit itself to upholding the basic instincts we share with them. This country is hugely dependent on its relationships with the wider world—in trade, for ideas and people, for education, and for the development of its skills base. Without that engagement the backwater beckons. Moreover, as most of you will know, the history of this country is one of engagement, of active and painful support for the causes and interests we share with our closest partners, and most particularly Australia. We cannot discard that inheritance.

Distinctive Australian and New Zealand nationalisms are probably here to stay. But that should not rule out a much greater effort in coming to terms with the realities of our situation—with the fact that we can complement one another's efforts, we can add value to what the other does, we can pool our resources, and together we can put our minds to working out satisfactory integrated solutions to the challenges which we face. Adding value does not mean integration or subservience. It means a rationalisation of resources in the military and other fields, so that the whole is more than the sum of the parts. It means defining the niches each party can fill in the overall, shared interest.

We should start by getting down off our respective high horses and by discarding the prejudices we have about one another. The smaller country will have to take the initiative to persuade the larger that it is truly committed to an Austral-asian partnership and can bring real value to it. Only in that way can we penetrate the layers of Australian indifference referred to at the beginning of this chapter. To make it work, however, an enduring, definitive, formal commitment will be called for, from both sides of the Tasman. In both countries we should perhaps be thinking more deeply about the words of Benjamin Franklin when the representatives of the thirteen American colonies signed the Declaration of Independence on 4 July 1776: 'If we don't hang together we shall certainly hang separately.'

CONTRIBUTORS

Roderic Alley was associate professor in the Political Science and International Relations Programme at Victoria University of Wellington.

Brian Easton is an independent scholar in economics, social statistics and public policy, and a Marsden fellow.

Damian Edwards was a policy analyst at the Australian High Commission in Wellington and is now a political adviser to the New Zealand First Party leader.

Jon Fraenkel is a senior researcher at the Pacific Institue of Advanced Studies in Development and Governance at the University of the South Pacific.

Alejandro Groppo is a lecturer in political theory at the National University of Villa Maria, Argentina.

John Henderson is associate professor in the Department of Political Science and Communication at the University of Canterbury.

Richard Herr is associate professor in the School of Government at the University of Tasmania.

Stephen Hoadley is associate professor in the Department of Political Studies at the University of Auckland.

Les Holborow is emeritus professor and former vice-chancellor (1985–1998) of Victoria University of Wellington.

Denis McLean is president of the Wellington branch of the New Zealand Institute of International Affairs. He is also a former secretary of defence, Wellington, and former New Zealand ambassador to the United States.

Malcolm McKinnon is a leading commentator on historical affairs and an independent scholar.

Terence O'Brien is a former New Zealand ambassador to the United Nations and former director of the Centre for Strategic Studies at Victoria University of Wellington.

Robert Patman is associate professor in the Department of Political Studies at the University of Otago.

Ralph Pettman is the professor of international relations in the Political Science and International Relations Programme at Victoria University of Wellington.

Keith Suter is a consultant at the Wesley Mission, Sydney, and senior fellow of the Global Business Network, Australia. He is also director of studies at the International Law Association's Australian branch.